Dearest Soul

Dearest Soul

A Spiritual Journey with Padre Pio

Fr. John Aurilia, OFM, Cap.

Our Sunday Visitor
Huntington, Indiana

"Lord, your love is everlasting"

(Jeremiah 31:3)

Padre Pio looking into infinity

Nihil Obstat
Msgr. Michael Heintz, Ph.D.
Censor Librorum

Imprimatur
✠ Kevin C. Rhoades
Bishop of Fort Wayne-South Bend
April 8, 2024

The *Nihil Obstat* and *Imprimatur* are official declarations that a book is free from doctrinal or moral error. It is not implied that those who have granted the *Nihil Obstat* and *Imprimatur* agree with the contents, opinions, or statements expressed.

Our Sunday Visitor Publishing Division
Our Sunday Visitor, Inc.
200 Noll Plaza
Huntington, IN 46750
www.osv.com
1-800-348-2440

ISBN: 978-1-63966-263-0 (Inventory No. T2932)
1. RELIGION—Christian Living—Spiritual Growth.
2. RELIGION—Christianity—Saints & Sainthood.
3. RELIGION—Christianity—Catholic.
eISBN: 978-1-63966-264-7
LCCN: 2024941336

Cover and interior design: Amanda Falk
Cover art: AdobeStock
Interior art: Piotr Wirkijowski

PRINTED IN THE UNITED STATES OF AMERICA

Contents

Part 3 — Non-Epistolary Writings

Introduction

Is another book about Padre Pio really necessary? There are already numerous books written about him. I do not know if my book is better or worse than any others, but I can say that it's unique, because what other people say — what the media and the world say about Padre Pio — is not as important as Padre Pio's own words. If you wish to hear Padre Pio talking about himself, about his relationship with God and people, you will find just that in the treasures of his letters written about one hundred years ago to his spiritual directors and to his spiritual daughters. I hope that you enjoy reading this book as much as I enjoyed writing it.

The saint's wish was that his letters be destroyed, unread by anyone. He wanted to preserve his privacy. Fortunately, somebody published some of his letters; but some had the wrong dates and there were quite a few discrepancies. In a corrective move, all 1,116 letters were published in three volumes. These letters were faithful to the originals and handled carefully, with professional accuracy.

For me, writing about Saint Pio is different from writing about Saint Anthony, Saint Francis, Saint Catherine, and the like, because I have never met them, or talked to them, or touched them, whereas I had the opportunity to do all of the above with Saint Pio.

Writing about Padre Pio is fun because his life is full of surprises, but it's also challenging because the padre has different approaches to different situations. The front cover of a 2022 Padre Pio calendar read: "The Faces of Saint Pio Giving Humanity a New Countenance." The pages showed Padre Pio contemplating, looking into the distance, raising his eyes to heaven, holding his head with his hand, smiling, kissing the image of the Blessed Mother, reading and writing, talking to people, celebrating Mass, being formally photographed, praying the Rosary, giving advice, and celebrating Christmas. Each "face" is truly Padre Pio, and yet all the faces point to one goal only: the glory of God.

This book started as a collection of conferences I gave in the United States and Canada. The development of the various topics was based on my understanding of Padre Pio's life, as I knew him personally. Later, I read the letters of Padre Pio and realized that my words and thoughts were inadequate in comparison with Padre Pio's words, by which he describes himself better than anybody else, including eyewitnesses; so this book took a new shape and form.

The first section outlines Padre Pio's journey as a prophet of our time, as one who is so similar and yet so different from us, and his involvement with the Secular Franciscans. While on earth, prayer and contemplation were the daily strength of his existential journey. Of course, Padre Pio had three outstanding "loves": the cross of Christ, the Eucharist, and the Blessed Mother. Mystical phenomena, obedience, struggle with the Devil, temptations, poverty, isolation and abandonment, humility, and devotion to the guardian angels were integral parts of his life and shaped his humanity and personality. Padre Pio was very much aware of the universal call to holiness, as stressed by the Second Vatican Council. In this context, I included the famous "Pray, hope, and don't worry," which was Padre Pio's most beloved phrase. The order or sequence of these topics is not logical, but simply casual. I wrote them as the Spirit moved me.

The first part of this book is 90 percent Padre Pio's words and 10 percent my reflections. You will enjoy the 90 percent because this section is Padre Pio's correspondence with his spiritual directors, Padre Benedetto and Padre Agostino.

The second section is made up of Padre Pio's spiritual guidance of his spiritual daughters, and I took the liberty to reprint one letter for each of them.

Some non-epistolary writings of Padre Pio conclude my work of love for our spiritual father, whom I personally affirmed to be a saint many years before he died.

Padre Pio reading the many letters he received

Part 1
Padre Pio's Journey

"Thank you for writing to me … trust in the Lord"

1

Padre Pio and the Secular Franciscans

Many books have been written about Padre Pio, but I haven't found any that mention the connection between Padre Pio and the Secular Franciscans. In his day, especially in the 1950s and 1960s, the Secular Franciscans were called Third Order of St. Francis — the first order being the Friars Minor, Conventuals, and the Capuchins, the second being the Poor Clares. The Third Order of St. Francis was made of laypeople willing to follow the constitutions stressing the spirit of St. Francis, but instead of leaving their homes and living in community, convents, and monasteries, they were encouraged to live a Franciscan way of life in their day-to-day lives. At the time of Padre Pio, every Third Order group was connected to, and spiritually directed by, a Franciscan friar. Padre Pio was directly or indirectly involved with Secular Franciscans when he was in Pietrelcina, Foggia, and San Giovanni Rotondo.

In fact, the structure of the Third Order gave Padre Pio the opportunity (in both a horizontal and vertical dimension) to develop two successful projects: the hospital called "House for the Relief of Suffering" and the Prayer Groups.

It's not possible to ascertain exactly how long Padre Pio cherished the idea of helping suffering humanity, for the alleviation of the sick in soul and body. We do know that on January 9, 1940, he confided to Drs. Mario Sanvico and Carlo Kiswarday his idea of building a hospital. After considerable difficulties were overcome, the work began on May 19, 1947. The building was blessed

on May 5, 1956, by Cardinal Giacomo Lercaro, in the presence
of over fifteen thousand people. Padre Pio at that time was very
much concerned about the poor farmers of San Giovanni Rotondo and neighboring villages. They had no medical facility for any
emergency. The nearest hospital was in Foggia, about forty miles
away. In many cases, people would die before reaching the hospital, given the shortage of transportation, both private and public.
At that time horses, donkeys, and mules were the best means of
transportation. The aim of the Secular Franciscans was to help
people in need, so Padre Pio brought assistance to their assistance,
in a manner of speaking, knowing that when we give an inch of
our love to God and our neighbor, God gives us a mile of blessings.

From the idea for a small urgent care facility, Padre Pio was
able to build arguably the best hospital in Europe with the generosity of people from all over the world. In the words of Padre Pio,
"The hospital was to bring relief to soul and body, to be a temple
of prayer and of science. This work is encouraged and pursued as
a practical call to the love of God through its charitable appeal."

The horizontal dimension of the Secular Franciscans was
very much alive in Padre Pio's life and is still very much alive, or it
should be, in every fraternity claiming to be Franciscan. The Franciscan spirituality of Padre Pio is the same as the Secular Franciscans who practice what they preach: compassion for one another.

In the presence of the poor and the needy, Padre Pio was
deeply moved and would willingly forego everything to be able to
help and console them. He wrote:

My very dear Father,
    May our Lord be always in your heart to sanctify
you. Five months have elapsed since I last gave you an
account of my conscience.[1] Since then the merciful Lord
has helped me powerfully by his grace. The Lord has bestowed very great gifts on my soul. ... Deep down in my

soul, it seems to me, God has poured out many graces of compassion for the sufferings of others, especially about the poor and needy. The immense pity I experienced at the sight of the poor man gives rise deep down in my soul to a most vehement desire to help him and if I were to follow the dictates of my will, I should be driven to strip myself even of my clothing to cover him.

Your son,
Fra Pio[2]

When we really love others in their sufferings, we love God, who wants to bring happiness and salvation to all. Whenever we help somebody, we bring him or her closer to God. It would be helpful for all of us if, at the end of the day, we could examine our activities and identify an act of love or an assist given.

Now let's mention the vertical dimension of the Secular Franciscans in connection with Padre Pio's spirituality. Possibly the project which most convincingly identifies Padre Pio as a great saint is the movement of the Prayer Groups. These began at the request of Pope Pius XII, who was having a tough time dealing with Europe during World War II and appealed to Padre Pio for prayers. Pio himself outlined the character of this movement in an address delivered of May 5, 1966: "It was to create everywhere nurseries of faith, furnaces of love, in which Christ himself is present each time the members meet for prayer at the eucharistic agape."

This was a small evangelical seed which soon grew into a big tree laden with fruits. By September 1968, 726 groups had been organized and were active in twenty-six countries with a total of 68,000 people, according to the guardian of San Giovanni Rotondo, Fr. Lino Barbati, OFM Cap. Today there are millions of people involved in this ministry. Prayer was the center of Padre Pio's life as well as of every Secular Franciscan's life. His prayer was liturgical, vocal, quiet, painful, joyful, but most of all, it was constant and grateful. Let us hear his own words:

> My very dear Father,
> May Jesus assist you always with His grace and make you holy. ... My usual manner of praying is this. I no sooner begin to pray than my soul becomes enveloped in a peace and tranquility that words cannot describe. The senses become inactive, except for my hearing, which is sometimes not inactive. Generally, however, this does not bother me in the least and I must confess that even if a great deal of noise were to be made around me, it would not disturb me at all.
> From this you will understand that I rarely succeed in using my mind in discursive prayer.
> It frequently happens that at certain moments when my mind wanders from continual thought of God who is always present to me, I suddenly feel the touch of Our Lord in a most penetrating and sweet manner in the depths of my soul, so that more often than not, I am obliged to shed tears of sorrow for my infidelity and of love for such a good and attentive Father who calls me back to his presence. At other times, I experience, instead, a great aridity of soul; I feel so oppressed by many bodily ailments that I am incapable of pulling myself together to pray, no matter how much I want to. [3]

Perhaps learning how Padre Pio prayed will help us to pray. I suggest the following: When you pray, God is the center, not you, and not others. As soon as you make God the epicenter, God will give you an important role in his vineyard. You are not simply a worker in his vineyard, you make a difference in the world. There was an old man who was complaining to God, saying, "The world is so bad, everybody is involved in crime, drugs, sex, and things are getting worse every day. God, are you going to do something about it?" God answered: "I did; I made you." Every prayer must be humble and sincere, always grateful. The prayer of St. Teresa of Kolkata may help us a great deal. In 1975, while visiting the Capuchin seminary in Lafayette, New Jersey, Mother Teresa prayed: "Thank you, Lord for giving me the privilege to serve my brothers and sisters." By helping others, we help ourselves spiritually.

2

One of Us and Yet So Different

The latest book of the Capuchin saints by Frances Courtright has the image of Padre Pio surrounded by many people on one side. From the other side, Jesus comes in with Padre Pio's guardian angel, walking toward the saint as a sign of approval of his ministry to others in the name of Jesus. The picture of Padre Pio in that book is the same man I encountered and lived with in the same fraternity as a personal secretary in August 1967. I can certainly say that Padre Pio is one of us, and yet so different. The great Pope St. Paul VI on February 20, 1971, addressed the Capuchin General and his council in these words:

> The miracle which will happen to you will be the same which happened to Padre Pio. Look how famous he was and people all over the world went to him. Why? Because he was a philosopher, a scholar, or because he was technologically updated? None of the above. The reason is that he celebrated Mass with humility, heard confessions from morning to evening and he was the representative of Jesus Christ in his prayer and suffering with the mark of the sacred stigmata.

We know that his vocation to our Capuchin way of life was inspired by a Capuchin brother who was begging door to door in his native village of Pietrelcina, working to feed the friars of the community. Francesco (Pio's baptismal name) was so impressed by that simplicity and humility that he asked to enter the Capuchin order and was received immediately. After a period of initial formation, he entered the novitiate in Morcone, Italy, where his baptismal name was changed from Francesco to Pio, as was then common in religious life. When he was ordained a priest on August 10, 1910, he wrote these words on the holy card: "Jesus, breath of my life, today with holy fear, I lift you up, in a mystery of love. With you, who are the perfect victim and the holiest priest, I want to be for the world the way, the truth, and the life."

A few years after his ordination to the priesthood, he went to Naples, Italy, drafted as a chaplain in the army, but he did not stay very long because of his poor and failing health. He returned to San Giovanni Rotondo, where he spent the rest of his life simply hearing confessions and celebrating daily Mass. The ministry of confessions was unique, something I found to be a daily miracle, because Padre Pio was hearing confessions for at least nine hours each day; once he said to us: "Today I feel really exhausted, I heard confessions for nineteen hours straight." The miracle for me was how feeble and frail Padre Pio was and yet that he could endure a schedule that would challenge a healthy person. Honestly, I can say that when I hear confessions for an hour, I need a break; if I hear confessions for two hours straight, I need a vacation. Padre Pio confided to his spiritual director, Padre Benedetto, the following words:

> My very dear Father, may Jesus bless and comfort you. I have not a free moment. All my time is spent in setting my brothers free from the snares of Satan. May God be blessed. Please do not afflict me further, like the others, by appealing to charity, because the greatest charity is that of snatching souls from Satan to win them for Christ. This is precisely what I am doing constantly by night and by day. I do not think any doctor from Barlet-

ta has come here. Innumerable people of all classes and of both sexes come here for the sole purpose of making their confession and I am only sought for this purpose. There are some wonderful conversions. Let everyone be satisfied, therefore, with a simple remembrance, as I constantly remember them all in Jesus' presence. I kiss your hand and ask your holy blessing.[1]

His way of hearing confessions was unique because he was abrupt and tough with some people and compassionate and gentle with others. He knew why and how to be one or the other. Once, I heard him screaming and yelling at a gentleman from Milan: "You, Dominic, go back to Milan and stop cheating, then come here for confession, now get out!" I note that Pio had never met this man before; how did he know his name, where he was from, and his sin?

Now, here is a pastoral point of view: If we priests do that with any person, we will be sued and the person would never set foot in any church ever. But with Padre Pio everything was different; people would come back in great number. That is the miracle of mercy, because Padre Pio used the tough love approach to bring people to God. In 2015, and throughout 2016, we witnessed the Extraordinary Jubilee Year of Mercy, when the Holy Father, Pope Francis, called to Rome priests from all over the world, dubbing them "Missionaries of Mercy," to hear confessions. Was that Pope Francis's idea or was it a prophecy of Padre Pio, who constantly said that "the Divine Mercy of God will gather and strengthen the flock around the shepherd?" And guess which saintly relics were exposed during the Year of Mercy at St. Peter's Basilica in Rome, Italy? St. Pio of Pietrelcina and St. Leopold Mandic, the two Capuchins who heard more confessions than any other priests in the world.

Speaking about confessions, the first time I went to confession to Padre Pio, I was shaking like a leaf, not knowing if he would yell at me. To my surprise, the first words he said to me were in Neapolitan dialect: "Uaglio' che' tremi?" (Boy, why are you shaking?) I said that he knew all my sins. He smiled so beautifully and said: "Is that what people say? I do not even know my sins, stop shaking."

Another insight of Padre Pio's confessions was the long line of penitents every day. Usually there were three priests in the old church also hearing confessions along with Pio. For all of us it was embarrassing because we had nobody in line, or one or two, and Padre Pio's line was very long. One day, we asked him why everybody went to him for confessions. With a good sense of humor he replied: "They think I am deaf."

Perhaps you know that going to confession to Padre Pio, reservations were needed. In my time at the Rotunda, the shortest wait time was twenty-seven days — if you were lucky.

Even though Padre Pio had a very heavy schedule, he was one of us, because he never missed the common meals or community prayers, and every day he would spend some recreational time chatting and cracking jokes with us, usually after lunch. He was one of us, and yet so different.

Another outstanding feature of Padre Pio's life was the way he prepared himself to celebrate Mass, the celebration of the liturgy, itself, and the thanksgiving after Mass. His Mass was at 5:00 a.m.; his preparation usually started at 4:00 a.m. He always had two assistants during the Mass — first because he could hardly stand up, but also to remind him to continue, especially because during the consecration and Communion he would stand still forever unless the assistant would gently poke him to continue. During the Mass, he would not wear the half-gloves, so the stigmata were clearly visible, and, at times, bleeding.

He did not permit photographs to be taken during the Mass, and I've wondered how there are so many pictures of Padre Pio presiding at the altar. Leave it to the photographers, I guess! At times, some people would say loudly "Miracolo, miracolo!" (miracle) or "Evviva Padre Pio!" ("Long live Padre Pio!"). The good padre would instruct the assistant to remove those people from the church immediately, making the point that Jesus is the focus of the Mass, not Padre Pio.

Many are struck by Pio's startling prophecy of his death in the context of the Mass. Let me explain: It was 10:00 p.m. and Padre Alessio bade "good night" to Padre Pio as he went to his room. On the way, Pio called to Alessio and said: "Tomorrow you'll celebrate the Mass for me." Padre Alessio jokingly responded: "You are kidding, you always celebrate the 5:00 a.m. Mass." Padre Pio calmly replied, "Alessio, you'll celebrate the Mass for me tomorrow morning." Padre Pio died at 2:30 in the morning.

When I was in San Giovanni Rotondo, I noticed something strange: Mass was scheduled for 5:00 a.m. The little church was old and in bad shape. It was not a parish; there was no church bulletin to announce the Masses; and yet every morning when we opened the church there were people waiting to come in, rain or shine, hot or cold. Too remote for vehicles, one could get there only by foot or riding a mule or donkey. How did so many people manage it? Pastors today try to fit their parish Mass schedules to accommodate people's needs, but there are always some who would say that the Mass is too early or too late, too long. Our pastors try to communicate with people as best as possible, but the printing of the bulletin is too small, the event was announced only once, and so forth. Yet there were many people every day at Padre Pio's Mass, simply because holiness is a magnet which attracts souls, because love is contagious.

Pio loved as Jesus loved. Believe me, you do not need a schedule or the bulletin to love.

3
Prophet of Our Time

The best book about Padre Pio was written by Padre Pio himself. It is called *Epistolario*, the *Letters of Padre Pio*, written to his spiritual directors and other people. By reading his letters we discover the real Padre Pio. Was he a miracle worker? Yes, but he was also more than that. Was he the priest with the stigmata? Yes, but also more than that. Was Padre Pio gifted with bilocation and languages? Yes, but also more than that. Was he the priest who could read hearts and minds? Yes, but he was still more than that. All of these things, though inspiring, do not make him a saint.

For me, Padre Pio is a saint — with all the traits of the traditional and contemporary saints — because he had the gift of contemplation and prayer, which overshadowed and gave support to any other gift. When he was a young priest and very frail from some still mysterious illness — to this day nobody knows what it was, but sometimes his fever would be so high as to break a thermometer — he was sent home to regain his strength because the Capuchin way of life in the friary was too rigid for his weak body, and at that time the provinces did not have infirmaries. During these long weeks, he spent his time praying, contemplating, and offering his illness for the healing of other people. His long period of illness became his strength because he was totally and completely dedicated to prayer, contemplation, and suffering. When he was discovered to have the stigmata, which he tried to hide for as long as possible, and people began coming to him from all over the world, he was told by the ecclesial authority not to see people, not to hear confessions, not to celebrate Mass in public. This isolation lasted for two long years. At that time, everybody around him was panicking; they believed he was being isolated and punished for nothing. Padre Pio made the best of it, though, immersing himself in prayer and contemplation.

Pio of Pietrelcina is a saint of our times. I say this because, as a military chaplain, however briefly, he understood the struggle of the war. He understood the struggle of the farmers and the unemployed, because he ministered to them for many years on the hills of the Gargano Peninsula. It was then that he conceived the idea of the *Casa Sollievo della Sofferenza* (Home for the Relief of Suffering) — he did not want to call it a "hospital."

While the whole world was looking for this saintly man, he was so humble that he was totally unaware of what was going on around him. He was not aware that he was the magnet for all kinds of people, good or bad, and he was so modest that his spiritual directors, Padre Benedetto and Padre Agostino, were constantly encouraging him:

> Dear Piuccio, I am very grateful for what you are doing for me and the Lord will not fail to reward your charity. May His resurrection bring you the desired fullness of light and remove you from the Limbo which precedes it. Bless the anxiety you feel and the physical collapse which follows. Remember the prophet's words "My body racked" (Ps 7:31:11) and you will have no fear. Your impatience is like that of St. Paul who exclaimed: "Who will deliver me from this body of death?" (Rom 7:24). Do not worry.
> Very affectionately in Jesus Christ.
> Fra Benedetto, Minister Provincial[1]

We love Padre Pio, because he was one of us, a person full of fears, conflicts, joy, pain, success, disappointment, and discouragement. We are indeed people full of conflicts and fears, whether we like it or not. A child experiences conflicts at an early age, when he or she must make choices, and some choices are not easy at all. We experience conflict along with fulfillment and happiness: We want to be what we cannot be.

Certainly, we are the choices we make, no more no less. What choices do we make every day? Padre Pio is a great master in guiding us through life, because he went through many tough choices: The "been there, done that" experience is the best book Padre Pio has written. He knew that God is in charge, and we none of us are saviors of the world (Jesus already did that!), that we all make mistakes, that we sin, we fail, yet he was able to make the best of everything. Conflicts did not break Pio; he broke them. His example demonstrates that conflicts do not make us weak, they make us strong. We do not like conflicts, difficulties, illnesses, discouragement, depression, but we have to deal with them, as Padre Pio did, not running away from them but facing things head on.

God is love, but nobody can do the work of love for you, you must do it. God is faith, but nobody can believe for us. And in our journey through life, nobody can walk for us, we must walk our path. As we come to know Padre Pio in his writings, we see that this is the greatness of the saint. He was really doing God's work as we are called to do as well. For many, Padre Pio personified the Gospel. To paraphrase an exhortation attributed to St. Teresa of Ávila, whom Pio reverenced: People do not read the Gospel, so you must be the Gospel.

Having lived with Padre Pio I have learned that I must do everything as if there is nobody else in the world to help make it better. I must love, and I cannot delegate anybody else to love for me, because the Gospel was not written for others, it was written for me. How many times, in reading its pages, do we relate it to the weaknesses and sins of others? We forget that the "Gospel for others" was never written.

The Gospels were written for you and for me, therefore we are responsible for what we do and do not do, always remembering that God is in charge and not us. In my office in the Bronx, I have a sign that stares at me every second: it reads: "Good Morning, John. This is God. I will handle all your problems today and I do not need your help."

Pio fascinated me because I could so clearly see Jesus in him, and in that way he became a Christ-image for me. This begs me to ask myself the very important question: Am I Jesus to others?

If people don't see Jesus in us, would we blame others? The horizontal dimension of Padre Pio was to embrace the entire world with all its good and bad qualities, all the joys and pains, success and failure. The vertical dimension of Padre Pio was his intimacy with God through prayer, ministry, and suffering.

I like to think about the life of Padre Pio as a garden, where there are violets and sunflowers. Padre Pio thought that he was a violet; I believe he was a huge sunflower, one who cared so much for the garden that he once said: "I will not enter heaven, I will stay at the door until all my spiritual children are in." You may understand that he was talking about the Prayer Groups, by which he started to renew the Church — not with extraordinary actions, but simply with prayer, humility, and good example. I like to quote our Holy Father, Saint Paul VI, who, addressing the Capuchin General Chapter in a private audience, said: "And now let's talk about Padre Pio, who was not only praying, but he was a prayer himself." The same was said about our holy founder, St. Francis of Assisi.

Padre Pio, in addition to being a contemplative person, was also very pragmatic and even playful. Once he paraphrased the Gospel by saying: "Man does not live by bread alone, but also, he does not live long without it."

Whenever I think of Padre Pio, what comes to mind is the

paradox or dichotomy of life: When Padre Pio was born, he was crying and everybody was smiling; when Padre Pio died, everybody was crying and he was smiling. Padre Pio has taught me with his example that life is a song: You write the words, God writes the music, because life is indeed a love story. Jesus, in fact, was born, lived, and died singing love. Now if we want the song to continue, we must do the singing:

Love.
Love always.
Love everyone.
Love everywhere.
Be a messenger of love.

4

Contemplation

Imagine Padre Pio's life as a garden, where you find different flowers, plants, vegetables, trees, shrubs, and thorns. This garden, however, has a section not open to the public. It is enclosed by a special wall, which we may call "mystical experience" or "contemplation." We do not know too much about it except what Padre Pio tells us.

What we know for sure is what Saint Pio described of his personal experiences in his letters to his spiritual directors. He did not intend to write a book of mystical theology, and so in his writings there is no external structure, which you may find in Thomas Merton's *The Seven Storey Mountain* or St. Teresa of Ávila's *Interior Castle*. There is, however, an internal structure, whether recognized or not by Padre Pio. According to his experience, there are eight sections in this secluded area, which happens to be the bigger garden area. After visiting the various sections of the mystical garden, we find an exit door, which does not lead us into reality, but into a mystery. Let us use Padre Pio's own words and the commentary of Padre Gerardo Di Flumeri, OFM Cap., who edited and published Padre Pio's letters.

PRESENCE OF GOD

The first section which identifies the mystical experience is the infused supernatural presence of God in the soul. Human activities and the effort of the faculties and senses are replaced by divine impulse working from within in the depths of the soul. The effects of this extraordinary and operative presence cannot easily be explained. The intimate relationship with God is so intense that the actions of the faculties become more and more vague. This contemplative step does not last very long until it reaches the limit of ecstasy. Padre Pio himself was not sure what was going on. Let us read what he wrote:

> This state of soul is becoming so intense that it will be a miracle of our Lord if I do not die in it. When the heavenly Spouse of souls is pleased to put an end to this martyrdom, He suddenly sends me an irresistible spiritual fervor. In an instant everything is changed, and I feel so enriched by supernatural grace and so full of strength that I am ready to defy the whole of Satan's kingdom.
>
> All I can say about this prayer is that my soul seems to be completely lost in God and that in those moments it gains more than it could in many years of intensive spiritual exercises.
>
> On other occasions I am seized by a violent transport, I am utterly in love with God, and it seems to me that I must die. All this comes about, not as a result of any consideration, but by an interior flame and by such an excessive love that if God did not come to my assistance I should in a short time be burnt up. In the past, by my own efforts I succeeded in calming these transports, but now I am unable to defend myself at all. What I want to say about all this, without fear of being mistaken, is that I by no means contribute to it. I feel at these moments that my soul ardently desires to leave this life and as this desire is not gratified, I experience a most sharp yet delightful pain, so delightful that I would like it to continue forever.
>
> It seems to me that everyone else finds consolations and relief in sufferings and that my soul alone remains in pain. The martyrdom which penetrates the

very depths of my soul is so far superior to its weak nature that it would be intolerable if the merciful Lord did not himself come to moderate the violence of certain raptures, so that the poor little butterfly becomes calm and quiet, both because the Lord has given it a foretaste of what it desires and because of other revelations He sometimes makes to my soul. I am also seized by a great desire to serve God with perfection. There is then no torment that my soul would not joyfully suffer. This also happens to me in an instant, without any previous reflection on my part. I do not understand the origin of the great courage I then feel."[1]

LOVE AND PAIN

The second section is "Love and Pain": Running parallel and together they accomplish a work of purification and transformation. At this stage, Padre Pio is overflowing with happiness and consolation. There are, however, painful intervals, which he calls "tricks of love." Of course, joy and consolation do not exclude suffering, but they make it bearable, desirable, and lovable. Padre Pio wrote:[2]

My very dear Father,

By God's will I still continue in very poor health. But what torments me most of all are the severe pains in my chest. At times these are so violent that it seems they must split my back and chest. However, Jesus does not fail every now and then to mitigate my sufferings in another way, namely, by speaking within me. O yes, my dear Father, how good Jesus is to me! What precious moments are these! This is a happiness for which I can find no comparison, a happiness that the Lord hardly ever allows me to taste except during suffering.

At such times more than any other, everything in this world wearies me and weighs upon me and I desire nothing else than to love and to suffer. Yes, my dear Father, even in the midst of great sufferings I feel happy, for I seem to feel my heart throbbing in unison with the heart of Jesus. Now, you can imagine what a consolation it is to know almost with certainty that one possesses Jesus.

It is true that I am subject to very great temptations, but I trust in Divine Providence that I may not fall into the tempter's snares. It is also true that Jesus very often hides from me, but what does this matter? I shall always endeavor with your help to stay close to him, for you have assured me that it is not abandonment on his part, but just the tricks of His love. Oh, how much I long to have someone to help me at such moments, to relieve my anxiety and moderate the flames which ravage my heart! Please be so good as to answer me, if you will and if you do not mind, to assure me of the truth of what I have told you so far. Recommend me to the Lord and bless me.

Yours,
Fra Pio

Greetings, thanks and all good wishes to Padre Agostino, the Father Lector, for all the good he has done me."[3]

Here is the reply of Padre Benedetto:

My beloved son,
I have neither adequate words nor feelings with which to thank the Lord for his goodness in treating you with such love and protecting you as he does. I see clearly that he has chosen to keep you close to himself, although there is no merit on your part. By this time,

you can be quite sure that He intends to take full possession of your heart which He desires transfixed by suffering and love like His own. ... Abandon yourself to His transports and have no fear; He is so wise, gentle, and discerning that He does nothing but what is good. Especially when interior delights are accompanied by a deep and tender humility, they must not give rise to any suspicion and the heart must be opened to receive them. Pray for me as I bless you with all my heart. Give my regards to the Archpriest and to the family.

Most affectionately in Jesus Christ,

Fra Benedetto,

Unworthy Minister Provincial

RAPTURE OF LOVE

The third section of Pio's contemplative life is the rapture of love, described as intense lights which the soul receives, and God's mysteries inundate the faculties and leave upon them an indelible stamp, although it is impossible to explain these things adequately to others. The soul suffers on this account and is unable to control itself so that it bursts out in laments and groans and cries of love, it leaps for joy and sings songs of praise, and so forth.

Here is what Padre Pio wrote:[4]

My dear Father, may the grace of Jesus always be with us. How am I going to make myself understood in what I must tell you? I feel the need to humble myself before the Lord to ask him, if He will, to guide my hand himself and give me the grace to succeed in telling you something of the great marvels which His mercy reveals to my soul. Dear Father, what a terrible thing is spiritual suffering! Miserable creature that I am, a holy trembling

takes hold of me as I start to deal with this subject, and
I am embarrassed by my utter failure to find suitable
words in which to explain myself.

My soul which is constantly receiving favors from
God, is not satisfied, and is continually groaning and
longing for its sufferings to be redoubled. As the days
pass, I see ever more clearly the greatness of God and in
this light which grows brighter, my soul burns with the
desire to be united to him by indissoluble bonds.

By this light I see how deserving this adorable Lord
is of our love and feel increasingly inflamed with love
for Him.

But dear God! This very desire to be united with
Him, to love Him as much as a creature can, causes in
me the keenest suffering, since I see more and more
clearly how far I am from the certain possession of Him
without fear of losing Him.

All this, however, is still tolerable and is nothing in
comparison to another fire which is blissfully spreading
in my soul. It frequently happens that when I am completely recollected, at the slightest thought that death
may be delayed in coming to unite me to God, suddenly,
I do not know how or from where, I am struck as if by
lightning, as if pierced through by a fiery arrow.

Alas! The wound I receive is far more penetrating
than the effect of lightning on the body! I am aware
that it has not been inflicted on that part of my being in
which ordinary pains are felt, but in the inmost recess of
my soul. In this state it is impossible for me to think of
anything concerning my own existence. From the very
first moment my faculties become inactive and have no
freedom whatsoever about the things of the world, except for things that increase and aggravate my torment.

The clear and keen awareness which the Lord gives
me of his lovableness and His perfections, of His goodness in pardoning those who have deserved nothing but
hell, increases my pain to such an intense degree that I
almost invariably cry out loudly.[5]

NEED OF SOLITUDE

The fourth section of his contemplative life is the need of solitude:

These desires consume my soul interiorly, since I understand by a most clear light given by God that I cannot
render Him the service I would like to give. All ends up,
then, in the delights with which God floods my soul.

Often, I find it very painful to have to deal with others, except those to whom one speaks of God and the
great value of soul. On this account I am very fond of
solitude.

Quite often I have great difficulty in attending to
the necessities of life: eating, drinking, and sleeping. I
submit to these things like a condemned man, merely
because God wills it.

It seems to me that time flies and there is never sufficient time for prayer. I am very fond of good reading,
but I read very little because my illness prevents me and
because, when I open a book and read a little, I become
deeply recollected and, instead of reading, I am immersed in prayer.

Since the Lord had begun to treat me in this manner
I feel completely changed, so that I do not recognize myself as the person I was previously.

I am clearly aware that if there is any good in me it is
entirely the result of the supernatural gifts. I realize that

this is the origin of my most firm determination to suffer all things with resignation and alacrity without ever tiring of suffering, although, alas, with how many imperfections! I most firmly resolve never to offend God even venially and I am ready to suffer death by fire a thousand times rather than knowingly commit any sin.

I feel I have improved a lot as regards to obedience to my confessor and to the one who directs me, so that I would consider myself almost damned if I were to go against them in anything whatsoever.

When I am unable at times to withdraw from conversations which are prolonged as a mere pastime, I must do myself great violence to remain there and I find this very painful. [6]

DEEP SENSE OF HUMILITY

The fifth section of Padre Pio's contemplation is a deep sense of humility. In this unitive stage, Padre Pio discerns a clear view of himself with all his limitations and unworthiness. Therefore, rather than attributing merit to himself, he recognizes and willingly acknowledges that all is pure grace of God. Here is how he expressed his feelings:

I fully recognize that there is nothing in me capable of attracting the gaze of this most tender Jesus of ours. His goodness alone has filled my soul with many good things. He hardly ever deprives me of seeing Him. He follows me everywhere, revives my life poisoned by sin, disperses the dense clouds which had enveloped my soul after I had sinned. [7]

My very dear Father, may the most sweet Jesus be always with you. I do not know what purpose can be served by the prayers of such a weak and sinful creature as myself who, as a crowning misfortune, is forgetful at every step of the graces received from God! I am completely useless. May the Lord have pity on me and since He loves me so much, may He make me capable of doing something for his glory.[8]

God is becoming ever more enlarged in my mind's eye, and I see Him in the heavens of my soul surrounded by a thick fog. I feel Him near me, yet I see Him quite far off. As my longing for Him increases He comes closer to me so that I feel Him, yet my longing makes me see Him farther and farther away. Dear God! How strange this is![9]

FEAR OF OFFENDING GOD

The sixth section includes the fear of offending God. This aspect is part of the so-called dark night experience. In the mystical journey of St. John of the Cross, the dark night is an "enviable state, because everything combines to dispose and prepare to receive the true form of the soul, which is nothing other than loving union." The soul can never attain to divine union unless it is first purified by the painful experience of the dark night. Only then, we can appreciate the light which comes to renew our soul and unite it to God himself. Knowing that Padre Pio is going through this uncomfortable experience, let us listen to what he says to Padre Benedetto:

What am I to say of my present spiritual state? The dreadful crisis of which I told you in my last [letter] is becoming more intensified. At present my soul is surrounded by a circle of iron. I fear, on the one hand, to offend God in almost everything I do, and this fills my soul with a terror that can only be compared to the sufferings of the damned. Do not think I am exaggerating, Father, when I make this statement, for this is exactly how things stand.

One night I recently felt I would die at the sight of this situation. The Lord caused me to experience the pains the damned endure in the infernal regions. What torments me the most, on the other hand, is that at the present time I feel an immense increase within my soul of the desire to love God and to correspond to his favors. At this point, Father, I prefer to keep silence, because I see clearly that what I have said and could say corresponds only very inadequately to what is taking place within me. Do you believe this, Father? It almost enrages me to be unable to manifest all that I experience internally. May the divine will be done. ... Praise be Jesus, who despite my unworthiness, desires that I share in His sufferings. Oh, my dear Father, how unbearable is pain when suffered far from the cross, but how sweet and bearable it becomes when it is offered close to the cross of Jesus!

Everything becomes easy for the soul, even when it feels oppressed and inebriated by every kind of suffering, and if there were not a basic fear in this soul of offending the divine Spouse, it would feel as if it were in paradise, such is the happiness that this manner of suffering brings.[10]

As Padre Pio comes out of the dark night experience, the light is not completely dissipating the darkness, so he experiences a sharp contrast between the desire to love God and the pain caused by people who do not love God, and that is the seventh section of his contemplative journey: lack of love. He writes: "Dear Father, if I could fly, I would like to shout, to cry out to everyone at the top of my voice: love Jesus who is deserving of love. But, alas, my dear Father, my soul is still strongly bound to the body, and many are the sins which impede the flight of my soul."[11]

On another occasion he wrote:

My very dear Father, may Jesus be the star which guides our steps constantly in the wilderness of this present life and bring us without delay to the haven of salvation!

With this most sincere and heartfelt prayer which I offer constantly to Jesus for you and for myself, I reply to your letter of September 27, which Father Guardian handed to me just a few hours ago. I firmly hope that Jesus will accept the pleadings of the one who confides to Him the entire care of himself and of all the souls most dear to Him.

What am I to tell you of my spiritual state? I see myself placed in extreme desolation. I am alone in bearing everyone's burdens and the thought of being unable to bring spiritual relief to those whom Jesus sends me, the thought of so many souls who foolishly try to justify their evil ways in defiance of the Supreme Good afflicts and tortures me. It causes me to suffer agonies, wearies my mind and rends my heart.

Dear God! What a sharp thorn has been driven into my heart! Lately I feel, to an enormously increased extent, at the apex of my spirit two apparently quite conflicting forces, namely, the desire to live to be of use to my brothers in exile and the desire to die in order to be united with my Spouse.[12]

REDEMPTIVE SUFFERING

The eighth section of this process is called redemptive suffering. His insatiable longing for great sufferings, his desire to repay to some extent the pains of the crucified God, and the cooperation with him in the salvation of souls are the components of the mission confided by God to Padre Pio. He is fully aware that his life must be a way of the cross and he wants to follow this sorrowful road with great generosity, embracing the cross from which he never wants to be separated and on which he desires to die. Let's see what he wrote:

> Recommend me to the Lord, you too, that He may not allow me to remain a victim to this common enemy of ours. I know that it distresses you not to have me close to you so that you could help me; but rejoice, Father, because I am happier than ever when I am suffering, and if I were to listen merely to the promptings of my heart, I would ask Jesus to give me all the sorrows of others. But I do not do so because I am afraid of being too selfish by desiring the better part, which is suffering. When we suffer, Jesus is closer to us. He looks on and it is He who comes to beg us for pain and tears, of which He is in need for souls. [13]

The redemptive suffering continues without any break, moreover it seems to increase, according to Padre Pio:

> I feel within me the great need to cry out louder and louder to Jesus with the doctor of grace: "Give me what you command, and command what you will."[14]
>
> Hence, my dear Father, do not allow the idea of my sufferings to cast a shadow on your spirits or to sadden your heart. So let us not weep, my dear Father; we must hide our tears from the One who sends them, from the One who shed tears himself and continues to shed them every day because of people's ingratitude. He chooses souls and despite my unworthiness, He has chosen mine also to help Him in the tremendous task of human salvation. The more these souls suffer without the slightest consolation, the more the sufferings of our good Jesus are alleviated.

This is the whole reason why I desire to suffer more and more without the slightest consolation. In this consists of all my joy. Unfortunately, I am in need of courage, but Jesus will not refuse anything. I can testify to this from long experience, if we do not stop asking Him for what we need.[15]

ENTER THE MYSTERY

The ninth and last section, "Enter the Mystery," does not have a specific topic, but it summarizes the mystical reality that cannot possibly be explained in words, but only lived and experienced.[16]

I feel my spirit liquefying, as it were, and sometimes to the point of causing me to faint. The flames (which are in no way like the flames of our material fire) beset and penetrate my soul to its inmost recesses and are so intense that they cause my poor soul pain and consolation simultaneously.

To tell the truth, although I feel these sufferings more terribly than death itself, I would never wish them to cease. This is a mystery which I cannot understand much less explain to others. Yet my soul is quite certain of what is happening to it and of all that goes on within it.

I have an idea of all this, or rather I see it with a most clear mind, and it is merely because I see nothing in this base world to which I could even faintly compare it that I find it absolutely impossible to manifest what goes on within my soul.

This causes me atrocious spiritual torment for I find no one who can understand me. But here a spontaneous question arises. If I am certain that this action is from God, why am I so distressed that no one, not even myself, can make things clear to the one who directs me?"

5
Humanity and Personality

I was fortunate to get to know Padre Pio by talking and living with him for a short period of time when I was answering the letters sent to him from all over the world in the month of August 1967. However, those who never met Padre Pio have the same privilege of knowing him almost as well as I did by reading his letters, sent to his spiritual directors and his spiritual daughters. I'm happy to begin with a discussion of his ordinary human traits as outlined in his writings: gentleness, mercy, friendship, sincerity, and thankfulness.

GENTLENESS
It seems to me that Padre Pio was not innately gifted with gentleness, but he achieved this virtue by way of constant and daily work. Let us hear his words:

> My ever-dear Father, may Jesus be entirely yours, may He transform you by His holy grace and make you more and more worthy of the divine promises!
>
> Your brief letter only reached me yesterday along with the salami and I hasten to reply to thank you for so much fatherly kindness, of which I realize I am less and less deserving the more solicitous you are for my well-being.
>
> Listen, Father, I am well enough aware of the tender affection you have for me, so I ask you not to embarrass me by sending me such things, especially when it means depriving yourself of them. All I ask of you is to be so

kind to help me always by your advice and your prayers. I do not need anything else and if I were to need anything I would willingly do without it.

You say that I threatened to think about myself alone. I do not know whether or when I said this and to whom I said it. At any rate, if I said it, I want you to know, dear Father, that it was not meant as you understood it. My way of acting is proof of this. I have worked and I intend to work; I have prayed, and I intend to pray; I have kept watch and I intend to keep watch; I have wept, and I intend always to weep for my brothers in exile.

I know and understand that this is not much, but this is what I am able to do and all that I can do. "Lady Gentleness" seems to be making progress in me, but I am not satisfied on this point. However, I do not want to lose heart. I have made many promises, dear Father, to Jesus and Mary. I want to acquire this virtue with their help and in return, as well as keeping the other promises I have made them. I have also promised to make this [the] subject of constant meditation and to suggest it continually to others.

You see, then Father, that I am not indifferent to the practice of this virtue. Help me by your own and other people's prayers.[1]

About gentleness, Padre says: "My only regret is that, involuntarily and unwittingly, I sometimes raise my voice when correcting people. I realize that this is a shameful weakness, but how can I prevent it if it happens without my being aware of it? Although I pray and groan and complain to our Lord about it, he has not yet heard me fully. Moreover, despite all my watchfulness, I sometimes do what I really detest and want to avoid."[2]

MERCY

Mercy and forgiveness are the hallmarks of Padre Pio's life and spirituality. It was not a coincidence that Pope Francis declared the year 2015–2016 the Year of Mercy, emphasizing that mercy "is the beating heart of the Gospel." Padre Pio's body was displayed in St. Peter's Basilica for public veneration. How strong was Padre Pio's compassion for others? Let us hear from him:

> When I know that a person is afflicted in soul or body, what would I not do to have the Lord relieve him of his sufferings! Willingly I would take upon myself all his afflictions to see him saved, and I would even hand over to him the benefits of such sufferings if the Lord would allow it.
>
> I see quite clearly that this is a most singular favor from God because in the past, although by divine mercy, I never neglected helping those in need. I had little or no pity in a natural way for their sufferings.[3]

And again:

> What am I to do? I do not know. I am suffering, I am seeking their salvation from God, but I do not know whether God accepts any of my groanings. Indeed, I may add that I doubt at times whether I even possess the grace of God. This most painful doubt is reinforced by the fact that I am in the dark as to whether the Lord accepts what I am striving to do to relieve the misery of others and by observing the continual aridity of my own heart, its restlessness and anxiety at the sight of so many suffering souls and my inability to help them.[4]

FRIENDSHIP

In spite of his natural temperament and character, Padre Pio shows deep friendship and affection for everybody. For instance, over his concern that he may be a burden to his brothers, he wrote:

> To the former trials of which you are already aware, there has been added a different kind of trial, the fear of being a burden and a trouble to everyone, especially to my brethren. There is hardly any foundation for this fear, yet it distresses and torments me and prevents me from enjoying spiritual peace even for an instant.
>
> This trial is so severe that in the past few days, at the height of my torment, the following words escaped me: "If I am a burden to you and my work does not please you, then tell me so quite clearly, for pity's sake, and I'll go elsewhere to ask for hospitality." Dear Father, you can imagine from what I have said how much this fresh trial is making me suffer. Since yesterday morning I feel more deeply wounded, but I am a little calmer and almost relieved of that deep dark torment. All this is due to the Lord's grace and the abundant tears I have shed.[5]

And on another occasion, he shows great respect for his spiritual director:

> Goodbye now, my dear Father, and who knows if I shall be granted the grace to see you again. I will not send you a kiss, because this is too little for all you have done for me, but I send you all that I have in my heart for you, which is an infinite tenderness. I hold you in veneration, Reverend Father.
> Fra Pio.

Francesco, my family, the Archpriest and all your friends send you infinite greetings and regards.[6]

Padre Pio apologizes for his "long silence":

> My very dear Father, do not take my long silence to mean that my love for you has grown less. The only reason is my sight which prevents me from keeping up a more frequent correspondence. However, I have kept you always present, close to Jesus. ... I have many things to tell you but must end here because my sight will not permit me to continue! Let my heart speak for me in the meantime.[7]

Is it not touching how he ends the following letter?

> With great warmth I embrace and kiss you, asking you on my knees for your fatherly blessing, while I remain entirely yours,
> Fra Pio, Capuchin[8]

SINCERITY

This virtue defined Padre Pio's personality, according to Fr. Tarcisio da Cervinara, OFM Cap.: "Tell the truth always, even if it may create discomfort." Padre Pio was strong in defending his points of view and in expressing, at times, disagreement even with his spiritual directors. Here are some excerpts from his letter:

> My dear Father, do not scold me for the delay in answering your letter; this is not due to lack of the will to write or indifference on my part. The reason is that I am out in the country to breathe a little more wholesome air which has made me feel better. ... You may imagine,

then, how I long to return to the community. The greatest sacrifice I made to the Lord was, in fact, my not being able to live in community. However, I can never believe that you absolutely want me to die. It is true that I have suffered and continue to suffer at home, but I have always been capable of performing my duties, something which was never possible when I lived in community. If it were a matter of suffering, well and good. But to be a burden and nuisance to others, without any other result than death, would leave me without an answer.

Moreover, I too have every duty and right not to deprive myself directly of life at twenty-four years of age. It seems that the Lord wills things this way. Think of me as more dead than alive and then do as you think best, for I am ready to make any sacrifice required by obedience.[9]

Again, on another occasion:

In your last letter you told me not to be egoistic, to tell people frankly the state of their souls, how they are to behave and how to love God. On this point I hardly understand you at all. At Jesus' school I learned that silence and hope are the strength of the soul.

But I never deliberately neglected to speak clearly to the souls God sent me; and if I have not been equally frank with my superiors it was because I considered reverence and respect required me to act differently.[10]

Padre Pio shows his determination about some miscommunication:

I am more than a little distressed by the fact that I have written several times to the Provincial, not without sacrifice on my part, and sent the cost of my medicines, but I have received no reply[11] — pardon me if I am lacking in respect on this point, but for the future I do not intend to send him the account for medicines. Let the Provincial use me as he thinks fit and as he pleases but let him leave in peace my family who are bleeding themselves for me continually and without complaining. Please keep this completely to yourself as it is just a son's outburst to his good father to relieve his feelings.[12]

THANKFULNESS

To say that Padre Pio was grateful is an understatement because gratitude was not a single act of kindness, but it was a way of life. He had an attitude of gratitude, something we see when we read parts of his letters in chronological order.

I have no adequate words to thank you as you deserve. But what hurts me most of all is not being able to show my gratitude in a practical way, as I should wish.[13]

I should be most grateful if you could manage to get me a little book entitled *Il Cappuccino ritirato* (*The Capuchin on retreat*).[14]

My very dear Father, *Te Deum Laudamus*, I have been able at last to read your lines. Your letter full of tender consolation has done good to my afflicted soul.

How can I thank you, my beloved Father, for being thus united with my sufferings even though this has sometimes brought you some consolation! I shall be grateful to you for your care of me and for the sufferings you have shared with me. I am most grateful for all this and hope to repay you a hundredfold when I am close to Jesus.

Oh, yes! I will then ask with holier insistence and

without false shame that graces be given for you. And if
I go before you do, as I hope, do not fear, for I will not
forget this promise.[15]

Convey my most sincere thanks to all those souls
who are praying for me and assure them that I remember every one of them without exception in the presence
of the Lord.[16]

On the same topic, Padre Pio wrote:

My very dear Father, may Jesus lavish more and more
abundant favors on you and make you ever dearer to
him!

I ought to have written to you sooner to thank you
for all you have done for me, especially the last time you
stayed here with us and for your deep concern for me in
my last illness.

Jesus, to whom I am constantly presenting you, will
reward you abundantly. Your advice, your suggestions,
and your fatherly admonitions by word of mouth are for
me so many immutable laws which with divine help I
am endeavoring to carry out.[17]

PHYSICAL CONDITION

There is no doubt that Padre Pio's personality is better understood in the context of his physical condition, which, at times,
shaped his human traits. Padre Pio knew that he was feeble, but
he never understood the origin and development of his illness,
neither could the physicians diagnose a convincing and satis-
factory explanation of the physiological facts together with the
appearance and/or disappearance of some symptoms, like high
fever and chronic coughing. Padre Pio himself did not believe
that he could be cured, but he submitted to medical treatment

willingly, or under obedience.

Let us learn more about Padre Pio's health, by reading what the Saint of Gargano said about it. Pio informs his spiritual director about his physical condition:

> You want to know the condition of my health, so here I come to satisfy you. Thanks be to God I have hardly vomited at all since Christmas, whereas previously I could retain nothing but water.
>
> I feel a good deal stronger, so that I can walk a little without much difficulty. But what refuses to leave me is the fever which pays me a visit almost every day towards evening and is followed by abundant sweating. My cough and the pains in my chest and back are what cause me continual suffering more than anything else.
>
> I ought to thank the Lord exceedingly for the strength He gives me to bear all these ailments with resignation and patience. For some time, I have felt that nothing here below attracts me anymore. The idea of being cured after all these storms sent by the Most High seems like a dream to me, indeed a meaningless phrase. On the contrary, the idea of death seems to attract me greatly and I feel I shall reach it before long. I do not know the reason for all this, and I turn to you for an explanation. [18]

The update of his physical condition continues:

> My very dear Father Provincial. Urged by the desire to let you have my news, I am sending you this letter.
>
> My general state of health is much the same, except for the fact that the chest pains seem to have become more persistent during the last few days. I am unaware

of the cause, and I silently adore and kiss the hand of the one who strikes me, knowing as I do only too well that it is He himself who affects me on the one hand and consoles me on the other.[19]

My very dear Father, for several days now my health has been much worse. But what torments me most of all are the cough and the chest pains. My cough is so severe and continual, especially during night, that it almost splits my chest, and I am frequently so afraid that I say the act of contrition. … Patience! It is true that I am suffering, but I am very happy in this state for you have assured me that it does not mean that God has abandoned me but rather shows the delicacy of His exquisite love. I hope that the Lord is pleased to accept my sufferings in satisfaction for the innumerable times I have offended Him. What is my suffering in comparison to what I deserve for my sins?[20]

Along with your letter I also received a postcard from Father Guardian of Morcone informing me that he had been instructed by you to accompany me to Naples for a medical examination. I am fully convinced, after your own assurance to this effect, that since my illness is due to a special permission of God that I do not need any doctors. I ask your paternity to withdraw the order given to the father guardian as regards accompanying me to Naples for an examination, for I too, like yourself who assures me of this, consider such an examination quite useless.[21]

While Padre Pio was in San Giovanni Rotondo and in Naples, he kept Padre Agostino informed about his health:

In January, as I told you in my last [letter], I had one

of my usual relapses. I had a very high fever and severe pneumonia. The doctor, poor man, considered my case to be desperate. And at the beautiful moment when I was beginning to taste the delights of the "winter is past" [Song 2:11], I was miraculously cured and cast out again on the deep sea to fight the good fight.

I was utterly disappointed, but then, Jesus permits it, and authority wants it, so I willingly resign myself to everything. However, about a week later I fell once more with the same ailment and the same prodigy was repeated. I have not resumed my usual occupation and I am fairly well, although very weak.[22]

On the 20th, I was examined by the commander of the company and by the chief assistant. Both diagnosed my disease as that already known to you, namely, infection at the apex of the lungs and on this account, they sent me to the observation ward where I remained until yesterday.

Yesterday morning I was examined by a captain and a major and they too pronounced the same diagnosis. With a view to further examination, I was transferred from the observation ward to the First Medical Clinic.

Here a further ten days will be required.[23]

6
The Eucharist

Of the Eucharist, there is little to add beyond the saint's own words:

> I have lots of things to tell you but find no words to express myself. I can only say that when I am close to Jesus in the Blessed Sacrament my heart throbs so violently that it seems to me at times that it must burst out of my chest.
>
> Sometimes at the altar my whole body burns in an indescribable manner. My face seems to go on fire. I have no idea, dear Father, what these signs mean.[1]
>
> I feel in my heart a great desire to tell you many things, all of them about Jesus, but I cannot express myself and my sight does not help me.
>
> Only God knows what sweetness I experienced yesterday, the feast of St. Joseph,[2] especially after Mass, so much so that I still feel it. My head and my heart were burning with a fire which did me good. My mouth tasted all the sweetness of the immaculate Flesh of the Son of God. Oh, at this moment when I still feel almost all this sweetness, if I could only bury within my heart these consolations, I should certainly be in paradise!
>
> How happy Jesus makes me! How sweet is His spirit! But I am confused and can do nothing but weep and repeat: Jesus my food! ... What distresses me most is that I repay all this love of Jesus with so much ingratitude. ... He continues to love me and to draw me closer

to himself. He has forgotten my sins and one would say He remembers only His own mercy. Each morning He comes into my poor heart and pours out all the effusions of His goodness. ...

Jesus asks me almost all the time for love, and my heart rather than my lips answers Him: "O my Jesus, I wish ..." and then I cannot continue. But in the end, I exclaim: "Yes, Jesus, I love you; at this moment it seems to me that I love you and I also feel the need to love you more; but, Jesus, I have no more love left in my heart, you know that I have given all to you. If you want more love, take this heart of mine and fill it with your love, then command me to love and I shall not refuse. I beg you to do this; I desire it.

Continue to help me with Jesus by humble and fervent prayer.

I am very distressed that I cannot say Mass, as there is no chapel and I am not permitted to go out. What desolation without Jesus![3]

• • •

What hurts me most, dear Father, is the thought of Jesus in the Blessed Sacrament. I have such a hunger and thirst before I receive Him that I almost die, and precisely because I am incapable of not uniting myself with Him, I am sometimes obliged to feed on His Flesh when I have a fever.

Moreover, instead of being appeased after I have received Him sacramentally, this hunger and thirst steadily increase. When I already possess this Supreme Good, then indeed the abundance of sweetness is so great that I very nearly say to Jesus: "Enough, I can hardly bear any more." I almost forget that I am in the world; mind and heart desire nothing more and sometimes for quite a long time even the will to desire anything else is lacking in me.[4]

I feel, dear Father, that love will vanquish me in the end. My soul is in danger of being separated from the body because it cannot love Jesus enough here on earth.

Yes, my soul is wounded with love for Jesus. I am ill with love. I continually experience the grievous pain of that ardor which burns but does not consume. If you can, tell me what the remedy for my present state of soul is.

This is just a pallid idea of what Jesus is doing within me. Just as a torrent carries down to the depths of the sea everything it encounters on its way, so also my soul, immersed in the boundless ocean of Jesus' love, by no merit of my own and without my being able to explain it, carries all its treasures along with it.

But, my dear Father, as I write, where do my thoughts fly? To the great day of my ordination. Tomorrow, the feast of St. Lawrence, is also my feast day. I have already begun to experience again the happiness of that day which is so sacred for me. Already this morning I began to have a taste of paradise. ... And what will it be when we taste it for all eternity? When I compare the peace of heart I experienced on that day with the peace of heart I have begun to feel since the eve of this feast, I find no difference.[5]

How important was the Eucharist for Padre Pio? A short answer is that the Eucharist was his life. Before people knew Padre Pio as the stigmatist, as miracle worker, as gifted with bilocation and reading hearts, they knew him by the way he celebrated Mass. His preparation for Mass would start at 4:00 a.m. with prayer and meditation. At 5:00 a.m. he would begin the celebration of the Mass, which lasted about two hours. During the consecration and communion, sometimes he was completely absorbed in contemplation to the point of needing to be reminded: "Padre, go on." Following the Mass, he would dedicate at least half an hour for thanksgiving. The Eucharist was a magnet that attracted Padre Pio in every way, shape, or form. I tried for a long time to discern what really made Padre Pio so attached to the Blessed Sacrament. After observing his way of praying and celebrating Mass, I concluded that the Eucharist for Padre Pio was food, mystery, and memorial.

EUCHARIST AS FOOD

The simplest and most primitive action of any human being is eating. The first thing the baby learns to do after birth is to eat in order to survive. What is true of the body is true for the soul as well. The soul cannot live without food: That is the simple explanation of Padre Pio's love for the Eucharist. For him it was a need, as ours is for our daily food.

As a good priest, Pio was very familiar with the Gospel of Saint John, chapter 6, where the apostle develops the theme of Jesus as Bread of Life.

For John the Evangelist, Jesus manifests himself in many ways. He reveals himself through historical events, like the exodus from Egypt, and the journey into Jerusalem. He reveals himself through the beautiful world of nature, a lovely spring day. He comes through people we meet, we talk to, or we live with. If you really go deep down in your conversion process, you find out that one of these elements is present in all of us. I am sure you can go back to a person who brought you to Jesus. Maybe you did not know his or her name, maybe you met him only once, maybe she is in your family or neighborhood. That person had an indelible impact on your life. That person may not be aware of that, but he or she was an instrument of God for you.

I cannot help thinking how many people Padre Pio touched and changed and he was not aware. All these ways are epiphanies of God, but the best way, according to St. John the Evangelist, is Jesus revealing himself in the holy Eucharist, because in all these events we receive part of Jesus here and there. In the holy Eucharist we receive the whole Jesus — that's why Padre Pio's relationship with the Eucharist is likened to Saint John presenting Jesus as the Bread of Life. This is a powerful moment for all of us: when we recognize Jesus as the bread of life. In our RCIA classes, I usually ask the inquirers at the beginning of the program: "What brought you here, why do you want to become Catholic?" Ninety percent answer, "The Eucharist. In our former religion or no religion, Jesus is missing in action."

EUCHARIST AS MYSTERY

Now comes the mystery: How is this presence made real to us? Padre Pio was very much aware of the mystery, and he was living the mystery rather than explaining it. Faith is the key to mystery, and, as we all know, faith cannot be explained; it can only be lived, because if we can explain faith, then we do not need faith at all.

Jesus did many things which could not be understood by his own disciples. Think, for instance, of the institution of the Eucharist: He went to the Upper Room, while his enemies were plotting for his death. Did the disciples understand that? Of course not. We live in a pragmatic society; we demand answers to all questions. How does it work? Why does it work? When no answers are forthcoming, it is more than we can take.

Padre Pio's spirituality was rooted in mystery, and he teaches us that there is an unbroken tradition of broken people. While we remain broken people, some more than others, we can break this tradition and we should. Do not solve the mystery, live the mystery, as Padre Pio did. When a friar asked Pio to pray for him because he was going to give a catechesis (explanation) of the Mass to a nearby parish, the padre answered with a broad smile, "You are going to explain the Mass? That would be a miracle, good luck!"

EUCHARIST AS MORE THAN A MEMORIAL

If you had the opportunity and privilege to assist at Padre Pio's Mass, you would understand what I am talking about. He was so immersed in the mystery that he was celebrating, that sometimes you could see a smile on his face or tears coming down on his cheeks. He was not simply celebrating a memorial service; he was indeed reliving what happened twenty-one centuries ago in the Upper Room and on Calvary. The Mass, in fact, is more than recalling something that happened long ago. In our vocabulary, remembering is merely the opposite of forgetting; in fact, it is holding something in mind. To the ancient Jews, remembering was much more meaningful: It was the bringing to life of past events. It was renewing and re-experiencing something which happened in the past. If you dissect the word *remember* you get "re-member," that is, to become a member again. When a husband and wife, together with family and friends, celebrate their golden wedding anniversary, it's much more than a memory. They do not simply recall that which took place fifty years ago, they relive it. They renew their experience of being together for another fifty years or more. Just so, Padre Pio's love for the Eucharist was in this context of reliving the mystery; it was more than a memorial.

7
The Cross

What distinguishes Padre Pio from other saints is his intimacy with the cross to the point of suffering, himself, with the holy stigmata. Some preliminary reflections on the cross may guide us to understand this prophet of our century.

Loneliness identifies the tragedy of the cross. The crucifixion of Jesus is the loneliest death in history. The government had labeled him as a revolutionary and rejected him, the religious leaders said "He was breaking the law of God," the Roman soldiers and the crowd mocked him and spat on him. Pilate washed his hands of his fate. The disciples hid in fear. Jesus was alone, hanging between two criminals. Therefore, when Jesus cried out: "My God, My God, why have you forsaken me?" he meant every word: He was alone. That was the greatest injustice, as well as the greatest tragedy, ever recorded in the history of the world. The tragedies of Greek literature fade in comparison with the brutal reality of the passion and crucifixion of Christ.

Padre Pio fell in love with Jesus crucified because of his humility: If Jesus, who was so perfect, suffered so much, then who am I to run away from suffering, from him, from the cross? I want to keep him company on Calvary.

There is a complementary sort of metamorphosis threading through Pio's life: Humility becomes love and love becomes humility. Since his childhood, Padre Pio suffered physically and spiritually. His constitution seemed frail. He experienced frequent headaches and debilitatingly high fevers. He suffered spiritually when sent home to recover because he missed the monastery very much and loved his religious community. Like other saints — Bernadette of Lourdes comes immediately to mind — Pio endured the great cross of being misunderstood and distrusted by hierarchs of the Church (and some of his superiors) about his ministry. Even in these struggles, he was able to imitate Christ in his "suffering alone."

Cardinal Siri, in 1972, said: "The first who must have recognized Jesus Christ were those who sent him to the cross; the same thing happened as well to Padre Pio." He was reduced to a reject, was segregated, prohibited to see people or even to go to church. For two years (1931–33), he was ordered not to have any contact with the faithful and to celebrate the Holy Mass in private.

Did Padre Pio like to suffer? No, he suffered simply for the sake of being one with the crucified Christ. He knew that the only way to be one with Jesus was to embrace him in his suffering; he knew that the way of the cross was not an easy one, but it was the only way for him. While in Africa, a famous missionary, Dr. David Livingstone, once wrote home to England requesting more workers. He received this reply: "We would like to send more workers to you, but they first want to know if there is a good road leading to your station." To which Dr. Livingstone replied: "If you are offering to send workers who will come only if the road is easy, I can't use them. I need workers who are ready to pick up their crosses and follow Christ, wherever he may be." The road to Calvary is not easy. There is no easy road to Christianity.

In the third millennium of our human history, we are all too familiar with the titanic battle that exists between good and evil and how times and terrors can begin to distort how we understand them, until good seems like evil and evil seems good — a perversion as real in our time as when the Prophet Isaiah said, "Woe to those who call evil good and good evil, who put darkness for light and light for darkness" (Is 5:20). Padre Pio is a valuable model by which to answer this ever-present dichotomy and paradox. When the Roman Empire declared war on Christianity and Christians were being arrested, executed, or fed to the lions, was it a defeat for Christianity? No. It was part of the great cosmic struggle that was going on between good and evil. Fortunately, this struggle made Christianity stronger. In the same way, Padre Pio's struggles, his difficulties with his superiors and others within his own beloved Church, made him stronger in his faith.

One of my favorite books, Herman Melville's *Moby Dick*, gives us the great white whale, symbol of virtue, holiness, and strength being pursued by Captain Ahab, symbol of evil. Ahab was determined to destroy the good. He failed. The classic film *Star Wars* developed the same theme: "The Force," the spiritual and supernatural way of the Jedi Knights, was good, while the Empire and Darth Vader represented the evil. They are engaged in a cosmic battle, and you know the end. But now, let us listen to the words of Padre Pio on this great, essential topic of good and evil:

> I am suffering, and suffering very much, but thanks to our good Jesus I still feel a little strength, and when aided by Jesus what is the creature not capable of doing? I do not desire by any means to have my cross lightened, since I am happy to suffer with Jesus. In contemplating the cross on his shoulders, I feel more and more fortified, and I exult with a holy joy.[1]
>
> Jesus tells me that in love it is He who delights me, while in suffering, on the other hand, it is I who give pleasure to Him. Now, to desire good health would mean seeking happiness for myself instead of trying to comfort Jesus. Yes, I love the cross, the cross alone; I love it because I see it always on Jesus' shoulders. By this time

Jesus understands my entire life, my whole heart is consecrated to Him and to his sufferings.

Ah, dear Father, pardon me for using this sort of language; Jesus alone can understand what I suffer when the painful scene of Calvary is enacted before my eyes. It is equally incomprehensible how Jesus can be consoled not merely by those who sympathize with His torments, but when He finds a soul who for love of Him asks no consolation and only wants to be allowed to share His sufferings.

When Jesus wants to make me understand that He loves me, He permits me to relish the wounds, the thorns, the anguish of His Passion. When He wants me to rejoice, He fills my heart with that spirit which is all fire, and He speaks to me of His delights. But when He wants to be delighted, He speaks to me of his sufferings, He invites me in a tone which is both a request and a command, to offer my body that His sufferings may be alleviated.[2]

I do not know what will happen to me; I only know one thing for certain, that the Lord will never fall short of His promises. "Do not fear, I will make you suffer, but I will also give you the strength to suffer," Jesus tells me continually. "I want your soul to be purified and tried by a daily hidden martyrdom; do not be frightened if I allow the Devil to torment you, the world to disgust you and your nearest and dearest to afflict you, for nothing will prevail against those who groan beneath the cross for love of me and whom I have taken care to protect."

"How many times," said Jesus to me a little while ago, "would you not have abandoned me if I had not crucified you? Beneath the cross one learns to love, and I do not grant this to everyone, but only to those souls who are dearest to me."³

Notice the power of this prayer in the following letter:

> Dear God! What has my life been in your sight during these days in which I have been completely shrouded in deepest darkness! What is to become of me? I know nothing, absolutely nothing. Meanwhile I will not cease to lift my hands towards the holy place by night and I will continue to bless you if I have a breath of life.
>
> I beseech You, O my good God, to be my life, my ship, and my haven, You have placed me on the cross of your Son and I am trying to accustom myself to it as best as I can. I am convinced that I shall never come down from that cross and I shall never again see a clear sky.
>
> I am convinced that I must speak to you during thunder and hurricanes, that I should see you in the burning bush, amid the fire of tribulations, but to do all this I see that it is necessary to take off one's shoes and give up entirely one's own will and affections.
>
> I am ready for everything, but shall I see you one day on Tabor, in the holy sunset? Shall I have the strength to ascend without growing weary to the heavenly vision of my Savior?
>
> I feel the ground on which I tread giving way beneath my feet. Who is to strengthen my steps if not you who are the staff of my weakness? Have mercy on me. O God, have mercy on me! Do not make me feel my weakness any longer!⁴

8

The Blessed Mother

There is a great connection between Padre Pio and the Blessed Mother, because Mary was the role model in Padre Pio's life; both lives defined the paradox between pain and joy, between God's plan and the world's plan.

MARY: PADRE PIO'S ROLE MODEL

The holy bishop Fulton Sheen said: "She existed in the Divine Mind as an Eternal Thought before there were any mothers. She is the Mother of mothers — *she is the world's first love*."[1] I remember the story of Fulton Sheen who was invited to speak in a rural church in upstate New York. It was winter and three feet of snow fell overnight, therefore very few people showed up for the morning conference, so the pastor said to Bishop Sheen: "I think we have to cancel tomorrow's conference, probably nobody will show up." The bishop replied, "No, do not cancel it. I promise you that tomorrow this church will be packed." So, he ended the evening conference by saying to the handful of people who showed up: "I understand that there are few people tonight because of the snow; tomorrow I will be talking about the woman I am in love with."

The next day there were hundreds of people, not counting the TV and radio staff. The conference, of course, was about the Blessed Mother. Was Padre Pio similarly in love with Mary? I asked him once: "Padre, how many rosaries have you said today?" Padre Pio, with a broad smile, replied: "John, I never count them."

I believe that Padre Pio was in love with Mary because she

was a role model for him, teaching him how to live a life that paralleled her own. Picture in your mind a young Jewish girl going about her daily chores: sweeping the floors, making the beds, doing the dishes, and being happy about it — thinking, "I will be happy for the rest of my life doing the will of God in all these small things."

That was her plan, but it was not God's plan. The angel of the Lord appeared to Mary and said, "You are going to become the mother of God." Maybe she thought, "You are kidding, maybe you wish to talk to the girl next door, she is better than me." But Gabriel assured her that she was God's choice, and she gave her consent, her fiat. As we know, her life changed because this holiest of humans knew that God was in charge, not her.

Think now, if you will, about Padre Pio's life: He simply wanted to be a poor friar praying and doing the will of God. That was his plan, not God's plan. He endured a chronic illness, which he did not want, but he accepted; the extraordinary gift and pain of the stigmata came along. He used to call the stigmata "thorns without roses." We usually want roses without thorns. He wanted to be a nobody, and everybody went to him for blessings and confessions, so he became a somebody.

Padre Pio was in love with Mary, because she was the woman who said yes to God without conditions. So was Padre Pio: "I don't want to be the center of attention, but your will be done." He did not like photographers in the church and in the friary, and yet he was highly photographed, even as he prayed the Mass. By obedience he stood before the camera ungloved because the Vatican required a picture of the stigmata. "Your will be done" was his echo of Mary's fiat and Jesus' prayer at Gethsemane. Though Jesus understood all that would happen, for Mary and Pio, in their humanity, it was different. Both said yes to God without understanding and without conditions.

THE MAGNIFICAT OF PADRE PIO

Just as the Blessed Mother proclaimed "the greatness of the Lord," in her most powerful proclamation of the goodness of God (see Lk 1:46), Pio's humility is similar. Like Mary, he does not say how great he is, but speaks only of the greatness of God.

In letters written to his spiritual directors, Pio stresses his smallness in the eyes of God. This is the very root of his greatness, and why I will argue that Padre Pio's Magnificat reflects Mary's own.

The Magnificat is not only beautiful poetry, it is an intensely powerful prayer of praise; it is revolutionary. It is a mission statement for the whole world, and it is for all of us. The human race has ever been divided into different classes: the privileged and the oppressed, the powerful and the weak, for "there is nothing new under the sun" (Eccl 1:9). Throughout history, the Lord has indeed confused the proud in their innermost thoughts, deposed the mighty from their thrones, and raised the lowly. Lowly Pio never intended to be the center of attention or to be important, quite the opposite, and because of that great humility, he really became great: Think of the Casa Sollievo della Sofferenza (Home for Relief of Human Suffering), think of the Prayer Groups, which spread in very short time all over the world.

The paradox of pride is that while we believe we are strong, pride has in fact made us weak. The power of humility is that it puts the Creator in charge, and before all else, and so all things are possible. This is why a proud person panics, falls into despair and depression when challenged, or when the illusion of strength meets reality. The humble person, on the other hand, remains calm and peaceful in any conflict, understanding that despite persecution, tragedy, and illness, they are not in charge, God is. The Magnificat of the Blessed Mother and Padre Pio teaches us that when we become set in our prideful ways and thoughts, we lose. When we embrace humility, we will ultimately win.

THE PARADOX OF MARY AND PADRE PIO

The tridimensional process goes on: Padre Pio was in love with Mary because she is the holy and perfect role model and because of their mutual embrace of the humility of the Magnificat. Now we consider the paradox between them.

Most of us, whether we think about it or not, tend to believe that life is easy, or life is impossible. Those two extremes were not in Padre Pio's vocabulary because consolations are never a constant. Mary said yes to God; therefore, was life easy? No. Think of the Flight into Egypt, the experience of missing Jesus for three days before finding him in the temple; think of Mary's sorrowful experience at the foot of the cross. Padre Pio said yes to God; therefore, life was easy? No. Think of his isolation, the pain of his stigmata, the suspicion of his superiors within the Church.

But Padre Pio did not give up. By following the example of the Blessed Mother, his life, though difficult, was not for him an unbearable negative. Pio made the best of things when he echoed Mary when she said, "Let it be done to me according to your word" (Lk 1:38). God was the center of their lives, not their egos, which we might think of as a system by which we "Edge God out." Connected with pride is the concept of happiness, which is not a destination to reach in our lifetime, but a journey and a process. Happiness is not "out there, somewhere," somehow external to us. Rather it is, "here, in my being" — a process of disposition and consent, a product of gratitude. The Christian principle of happiness is "Nobody makes me happy; nobody makes me sad; I alone do this." We understand, then, why Padre Pio kept his good sense of humor (as can we) even through struggles and difficulties. Saint Pio and the Blessed Mother both were oriented toward God, as servants of the Christ. They knew where they were going, and the conflicts became opportunities rather than obstacles.

I, personally, find the prayer of Thomas Merton, from *Thoughts in Solitude,* extremely useful when pondering this truth:

> My Lord God,
> I have no idea where I am going.
> I do not see the road ahead of me.
> I cannot know for certain where it will end.
> Nor do I really know myself,
> and the fact that I think that I am following your will
> does not mean that I am actually doing so.
> But I believe that the desire to please you
> does in fact please you.
> And I hope I have that desire in all that I am doing.
> I hope I will never do anything apart from that desire.
> And I know that if I do this you will lead me by the
>   right road
> though I may know nothing about it.
> Therefore, I will trust you always though
> I may seem to be lost and in the shadow of death.
> I will not fear, for you are ever with me,
> and you will never leave me to face my perils alone.

Now let's hear from Padre Pio:

> I am indebted to our Mother Mary for driving away the temptations. Will you too, please, thank the good Mother for these exceptional graces which she obtains for me at every moment, and meanwhile please suggest to me some means by which I can in all things please this Blessed Mother?
>
> The greatest sign of love you can show me will be precisely this, that you too thank our Blessed Lady for me.
>
> My dear Father, oh, the lovely month of May! It is

the most beautiful month of the year. Yes, dear Father, how well this month preaches the tenderness and beauty of Mary! When I think of the innumerable benefits received from this dear Mother, I am ashamed of myself, for I have never sufficiently appreciated her heart and her hand which have bestowed these benefits upon me with so much love, and what troubles me most is that I have repaid the affectionate care of this mother of ours by continually offending her.

How often have I confided to this mother the painful anxieties that troubled my heart! And how often has she consoled me! But in what did my gratitude consist? In my greatest sufferings it seems to me that I no longer have a mother on this earth, but a very compassionate one in heaven. But many times, when my heart was at peace, I have forgotten all this almost entirely. I have even forgotten my duty of gratitude towards this blessed heavenly Mother!

For me, the month of May is a month of graces and this year I am hoping for just two. The first is that she should take me to herself, or else, if I am to go on living, that all the consolations of this world be changed into sufferings for me if she will only prevent me from seeing any more the wicked faces of those. ... The other grace I desire is that she obtain for me ... you know what I mean, dear Father."[2]

I do not dare to ask her for this latter grace, because if it displeased her, she would hide her lovely face from me again as she has done on other occasions.

Poor dear Mother, how you love me! I observed it once more at the dawn of this beautiful month. What great care she took to accompany me to the altar this morning. It seemed to me that she had nothing else to think about but me, filling my heart with holy sentiments.

I felt a mysterious fire in my heart which I could not understand. I felt the need to put ice on it, to quench this fire which was consuming me.

I wish I had a voice strong enough to invite the sinners of the whole world to love Our Lady. But since this is not within my power, I have prayed and will pray to my dear Angel to perform this task for me. [3]

We know that Padre Pio had great devotion to Our Lady of Grace, patroness of the church in San Giovanni Rotondo, but we learn here that he was devoted to the Sorrowful Mother as well:

May the Sorrowful Virgin obtain for us from her most holy Son the grace to penetrate more deeply into the mystery of the cross and like her to become inebriated with Jesus' sufferings. … May the most holy Virgin obtain for us love of the cross, love of pain and suffering and may she who was the first to practice the gospel in all its perfection before it was written, enable us and stimulate us to follow her example. Let us not refuse to take this path, we who want to reach our journey's end. Let us invariably unite with this dear Mother. With her, close to Jesus, let us go out from Jerusalem, the symbol and figure of Jewish obduracy, of the world which rejects and denies Jesus Christ and from which Jesus Christ declared himself to be separated when he said: "I am not of this world" (Jn 8:23) and which He excluded from His prayer to the Father: "I am not praying for the world" (Jn 17:9).[4]

9
Pray, Hope, and Don't Worry

The Bible reflects geometry quite often. For instance, the circle is the symbol of perfection and completeness because there is no end or beginning, but simply a flowing continuum. The circle in the Bible is dynamic, not static. The power of the triangle comes from relationship; if the dimensions are not connected or one dimension is missing, there is no triangle, there is no power; there is only chaos. In Padre Pio's life he was known to utter a most successful triangle — "Pray, hope, and don't worry" — which is very much related to the power triangle (God, others, yourself).

PRAY
It seems to me that Padre Pio's motto "Pray, hope, and don't worry" is succinct advice on how to make our existential journey meaningful. According to him, prayer is always the key, not only because "It opens the door to heaven" (using his words), but it is the cornerstone of our Christian lives. On December 8, 1912, Padre Benedetto wrote the following letter to somebody (addressee unknown), and this letter was found in Padre Pio's collection. Perhaps Pio used it as a guide for himself, and guidance for others. Here is the text:

> Beloved soul in Christ, I come at once to the point:
>   When the soul enjoys the Supreme Good and remains in deep and peaceful recollection, the prayer is good and is called the "prayer of quiet."

In this state, the soul is not subject to illusions and deception as in vision, etc., in which the senses are involved, because here all is spiritual.

Hence, we should not resist grace, but second it by allowing it to act peacefully.

The soul favored with such a gift should try to understand and feel what God wants without being distracted by thinking about what is happening within him and how it comes about. He should merely recommend himself and others by short prayers to the divine mercy.

In this state of soul, he should merely pay attention to whether, when this recollection is over, he feels his heart replenished with charity and his intellectual and physical faculties renewed, because this is the sure sign that it is God who is operating within him.

It is well to prepare oneself humbly and tranquilly for one's prayer, for if one is sometimes taken by surprise and plunged into recollection, this is all to the good and there is a greater certainty that it is God who is acting in the soul.

The time spent in such prayer is not wasted, for according to what has been said, it is not a question of being stupefied, but of a tranquil activity in the faculties which have been seized by God and, although this action is very gentle, it is nonetheless active.

It is one thing to be at a standstill, but it is another to travel by a fast train which runs so smoothly that one seems to be at a standstill, while one covers great distances in a very short time. May I ask you to say the rosary of Our Lady for me and to get others to pray for me as requested and promised during the retreat.

By reading the many letters Padre Pio wrote to his spiritual directors and to his spiritual daughters, we can say that Padre Pio's prayer was joyful, painful, contemplative, active, verbal, mental, and constant.

HOPE

By experience, we know that hope comes into play when crisis appears, opening us up to "best possibilities." When one door closes, goes the cliché, another door opens.

Hope works as follows: Adversity triggers our minds to find a solution and imagination forms in tandem, which takes some risks, identifies the negative and positive, and chooses the positive, also called "hope."

Those familiar with Greek mythology may remember Prometheus, who stole fire from the god Zeus, who was furious. Zeus tried to get even by placing all the evils in a box, which he gave to Pandora to give to Prometheus. Pandora was told not to open the box, but she did, so all the evils were released into the world. Hope, which was hiding at the bottom, in the dark, remained. So, as the saying goes: When everything else fails, there is still hope.

I like to quote a phrase from Alexander Pope's *Essay on Man*: "Hope springs eternal in the human breast: Man never is, but always blest." I am sure you remember in *Star Wars* the character Luke Skywalker, who works for good to triumph over evil. Before Star Wars and all the modern thinkers writing on hope, Saint Paul's theology assures us that we may overcome evil with good (see Rom 12:21).

Padre Pio was spending some time in his hometown of Pietrelcina for health reasons when he wrote this letter: "Bear with your exile for the sole reason that God wills it. What a great advantage this is for you. O my Jesus, I will live this cruel life and hope and silence will be my strength if this wretched life lasts. Meanwhile, O my Creator and my God, make this bright flame of your love burn ardently in my heart."[1]

We can see clearly that hope relates to suffering and faith, which make hope stronger and long-lasting. About a month later from the previous letter, Padre Pio wrote about the same topic:

> Then it is that my soul, resting in God, feels such a great aversion for this repose that I almost faint, for I would willingly sacrifice the delights of my soul's repose if I might hope to enkindle in others the desire for this happiness which makes one blessed. ... I am oppressed by the uncertainty of my future, but I cherish the lively hope of seeing my dream fulfilled, because the Lord cannot place thoughts and desires in a person's soul if He does not really intend to fulfill them, to gratify these longings which He alone has caused.[2]

When Padre Pio talks about his future, he really means if and when he can return to the fraternity. Can you imagine how painful it must have been to celebrate the feast of St. Francis of Assisi outside the cloister, without his Capuchin brothers?

God in his Providence permitted Padre Pio to go back into the friary in San Giovanni Rotondo, but while still facing challenges in his spiritual and physical journey:

> May I hope for mercy and that he will listen at last to my cries, or must I give up this hope? Dear God. ... When the storm is at its height and my excessive misery is crushing me, I have hardly any faith left. I am powerless to lift myself up on the wings of hope, a virtue so necessary for abandonment in God. I have no charity. For to love my God is the consequence of all awareness in active faith, into whose promises the soul plunges to be refreshed and to abandon itself to repose in sweet hope.[3]

This letter is ten pages long, because Pio really goes into detail about suffering and hope. For the saint, suffering is real, but hope is the opposite of giving up.

> Where am I wandering? The difficulty of my state appears insurmountable to me, especially in these days of more refined torment. Where on earth am I rushing headlong? I am on no path; I am completely and perhaps irreparably lost. I know no means, I receive no last ray of light, not a glimmer; no rule, no life or truth to be learned which could sustain and revive me and enable me to hope against hope as you suggested to me.[4]

To hope against hope is something we all experience at some time in our life. The teaching of Padre Pio is very pragmatic here, telling us that hope is always more powerful than despair, in which hope is cast away.

DON'T WORRY

Though hope and prayer anticipate the positive in every occasion, anxiety (worry) focuses on what is negative. We usually worry because we imagine (and want to avoid) anticipated threats or troubles, and this adds to our stress. Hope, when it is sincere, generates peace. The emotional state of being worried about a real or imagined personal, financial, spiritual, or emotional issue can paralyze us completely, whereas prayer and hope make us free.

Should we worry about things and people? Padre Pio, as we read in his letters, did worry about some people, events, and situations. So, when Padre Pio says, "don't worry," he means don't worry excessively, or unto despairing, but, yes, we are human and our nature allows for concern about things like using prudence and safety, or avoiding risky behavior, or in our concerns for the good of another. Psychologists tell us to stay away from toxic worry, to talk to people rather than worry alone in one's imagination, and to not make decisions when we are worried. We often worry because of the experience of a paradoxical dichotomy between what we want to achieve and what we don't achieve, and we forget that happiness is not a goal, but a process; it's not a destination, but it's the journey itself.

The wishful thinking whereby we make our plans, "when I … then I will …" rarely works out as we'd envisioned. In his letters we see that Padre Pio is sometimes worried about not being able to love God as much as possible, being away from the religious house, and not being able to celebrate Christmas, which he loved, with the friars of the Capuchin monastery. "Living here below is wearisome to me, my dear Father. It is such a bitter torment to me to live in exile that I can hardly go on any longer. The thought that at any moment I may lose Jesus, distresses me in a way that I cannot explain; only a soul that loves Jesus sincerely can understand what this means."[5]

Padre Agostino was in Udine, a city in northeastern Italy, for military service when he wrote an encouraging letter:

Meanwhile, how is your spiritual life? Always the same? Are you always in darkness? Always distressed? Are you convinced that your state is as Jesus wants it? Believe at least the word of authority which does not intend to deceive you and cannot do so because God has established it for the guidance of souls.

Be of good heart, my dear son: It is Jesus who wants you to be in this state, but He is with you, have no doubt about it. If it were not Jesus, you would be lost, as you would be unable by yourself to overcome all the trials of your life.

Another trial is now approaching, the repetition of the medical examination. Let us trust in the help of Jesus and His Immaculate Mother.[6]

Yet, even after this letter of encouragement, Padre Pio was still worried.

Believe me, this is the highest peak of my interior martyrdom. I am living in a perpetual night and the darkness is often deepest. I long for light and this light never comes; and if at times a feeble ray is visible, which happens only too seldom, this itself arouses once more in my soul the most desperate longing to see the sunshine again; my longing is so strong and violent that it very often makes me languish and pine for love of God and I find myself on the verge of fainting.

I experience all this without wanting it or making any effort to bring it about. Often, it all happens to me outside the times of prayer and even when I am occupied in different actions.

I have no desire to experience these things, because I realize that when they are very violent, they affect my body also and I am very much afraid that this is not a divine operation. Ah, Father, you cannot imagine what this fear means to me. I feel I am dying at each moment, and I wish I could die so as not to feel God's hand weighing heavily on my soul.

What on earth is this? How am I to act to get out of such a deplorable state? Is it God who is acting in me or is it someone else? Speak to me frankly, as usual, and explain to me how all this comes about.[7]

Padre Pio was indeed worried on many occasions, but because of his great sense of hope and his constant prayer, was able to perform his ministry and help others who were worried, lest they fall into despair. In fact, he wrote Letter 397 to his spiritual director, Padre Agostino, who was then in the Italian Army and was then very worried about what was happening during the war:

> My very dear Father, may Jesus be in the center of your heart and set it all on fire with His divine love!
>
> I invariably praise and bless God for His continual assistance in your regard and for the way He helps you to bear your trials without wavering. All the same, my dear Father, I observe in you some slight anxiety and longing which hinder the full effect of your patience. "By your patience you will possess your souls" [Lk 21:19] the Divine Master tells us. It is therefore through patience that we will possess our souls, and to the extent to which it is perfect will the possession of our souls be entire, perfect, and certain, hence, the less it is mixed with longings and anxiety, the more perfect is our patience. You are suffering because you are in exile, you have borne for a year the inconvenience which war brings with it and now you are longing for rest; but remember this, that the children of Israel remained for forty years in the desert before taking possession of the Promised Land, although only a few weeks were required for the journey. Yet it was not lawful to investigate the reasons why God postponed their entry into possession of that land and those who murmured about it died without setting foot there. Moses himself, the servant of God, died on the frontier of the Promised Land which he saw from a distance but was never able to enjoy. Courage, then, my dear Father, and carry on peacefully. Jesus will invariably help you. Exile according to God's will be better than the tabernacles of Jacob without his will.[8]

10
The Angels

Padre Pio had a great devotion to the angels. We know, in fact, that he traveled to Monte Sant'Angelo to visit the shrine of St. Michael the Archangel:

> Dearest Assunta,
> May the Lord be with you always, and may He comfort and help you in the hour of trial.
> Make allowances for me if am unable to reply in a fully satisfactory manner to your letter, for reasons easily understood. I will do so as soon as I can and when I feel well again after the fatigue of the trip I made yesterday to Monte Sant'Angelo, to visit Saint Michael. Meanwhile, be patient and live peacefully without fearing the snares of Satan, who would like to see you lost if that were possible.[1]

Padre Pio's life is filled with angels, but there is something peculiar about his relationship with his guardian angel. I will try to outline some instances in which his guardian angel is not only present in his life, but very active and busy. The guardian angel translated or wrote French and Greek for him, because he knew neither language.

We know from their mutual correspondence that Padre Agostino asserts that Padre Pio knew neither Greek nor French. His guardian angel explained everything to him, and he replied appropriately. In fact, the last sentence of the letter written on August 26, 1912, to Padre Agostino from Pietrelcina and the entire letter of

Padre Pio to Padre Agostino written from Pietrelcina were written in French.

Padre Agostino asks: "If possible, will you satisfy my curiosity. Who taught you French? How is it that while you didn't like it before, you like it now?"[2]

Padre Pio gives a biblical answer: "To your question about the French language, I reply with Jeremiah: Ah, Lord God, *'Nescio loqui.'*"[3]

On September 7, 1912, Padre Agostino wrote to Padre Pio from Foggia a whole letter in Greek. At the foot of the letter the parish priest of Pietrelcina wrote the following testimony: "Pietrelcina, August 25, 1919. I, the undersigned, testify under oath that when Padre Pio received this letter, he explained its contents to me literally. When I asked him how he could read and explain it as he did not know even the Greek alphabet, he replied: 'You know! My Guardian Angel explained it all to me.' Signed by the Archpriest, Salvatore Pannullo."

The guardian angel told him to sprinkle the letters with holy water:

> With the help of the good angel, that wretch has been vanquished this time in his wicked design and your letter has been read. The Angel had suggested to me to sprinkle your letters with holy water before opening them. I did this with your last but cannot tell you how enraged the ogre was! He wants to put an end to me at all costs and is using all his diabolical cunning to this end. But he will be crushed. The Angel assures me of this, and paradise is with us.[4]
>
> The heavenly beings continue to visit me and to give me a foretaste of the rapture of the blessed. And while the mission of our Guardian Angels is a great one, my own Angel's mission is certainly greater since he has the addi-

tional task of teaching me other languages.[5]

His guardian angel also had the task of giving him a wakeup call. "Again, at night when I close my eyes the veil is lifted and I see paradise open up before me; and gladdened by this vision I sleep with a smile of sweet beatitude on my lips and a perfectly tranquil countenance, waiting for the little companion of my childhood to come to waken me, so that we may sing together the morning praises to the beloved of our hearts."[6] Isn't it fascinating that his angelic companion from childhood not only woke him up, but prayed with him at Morning Prayer?

When the Devil beat Padre Pio, here is what he said:

> I cannot tell you the way these scoundrels (devils) beat me. Sometimes I feel I am about to die. On Saturday it seemed to me that they intended to put an end to me and I did not know what saint to invoke. I turned to my Angel and after he had kept me waiting for a while, there he was hovering close to me, singing hymns to the divine Majesty in his angelic voice. There followed one of the usual scenes; I rebuked him bitterly for having kept me waiting so long when I had not failed to call him to my assistance. To punish him, I did not want to look him in the face. I wanted to get away, to escape from him. But he, poor creature, caught up with me almost in tears and held me until I raised my eyes to his face and found him all upset. Then: "I am always close to you, my beloved young man," he said, "I am always hovering around you with the affection aroused by your gratitude to the Beloved of your heart. This affection of mine will never end, not even when you die."
>
> Poor little Angel! He is too good. Will he succeed in making me appreciate the serious duty of gratitude?[7]

11
Humility

Saint Luke makes a paradoxical statement: "But when Jesus perceived the thought of their hearts, he took a child and put him by his side, and said to them, 'Whoever receives this child in my name receives me, and whoever receives me receives him who sent me; for he who is least among you all is the one who is great'" (Lk 9:47–48). To better understand this statement, we must read the Beatitudes: Blessed are the poor because they are rich, blessed are those who suffer, because they will rejoice. It seems to me that children are not humble — they brag about everything — but Jesus is fascinated with them because they are authentic: What you see is what you get. Humility is simple reality. Humility tells us, "Drop the mask. Show your real face!" (It's better than you think!) Actors in the Greek comedies and tragedies used masks made of wax to impersonate different characters. They were not what seemed to be. Christians are not actors; we are not even spectators of the game: we play the game unmasked. Let us be sincere, then we are humble. The adjective *sin-cere* comes from the Latin *sine-cera* — meaning "without wax." I can say that Padre Pio was much like a child, yet he also believed he was the worst human being on the face of the earth, and I believe that is exactly the reason why he was like a magnet, especially to grave sinners. Everybody was attracted to Pio because he was real and humble. The fact that he was endowed with supernatural gifts did not make him proud, but humble. His daily life was marked by sincerity and frankness towards God, his spiritual directors, and the people he encountered.

For Padre Pio, humility became a bond of unity with the

sinners who sought him out and a challenge for those who were sincerely searching for faith, hope, and love. Divisions among Christians and non-Christians did not come from God; they came from us. Christian humility is and must be a reality of life, rather than a resemblance of goodness. We are never so powerful as when we are humble; we are never so powerful as when we are on our knees.

Now, let us hear from Padre Pio himself about humility:

> My very dear Father, with bitter tears in my eyes and with trembling hand I am writing this to ask your pardon on my knees for all I have done to offend you with such impudence. I am sorry for all this, as one in love with God is sorry for his sins.
>
> Ah, forgive me, dear Father. I realize that I do not deserve forgiveness, but your goodness induces me to hope for it. Do not be upset. Don't you know that I am full of pride? Let us pray together that the Lord may strike me dead before I go to such extreme again.[1]

I am not sure what triggered this act of contrition, but I presume that it was a minor disagreement with his spiritual director.

> I never failed to receive remarkable benefit from the supernatural things which have happened to me. These heavenly favors, apart from the effects proper to each favor, have produced within me three principal effects: an admirable knowledge of God and of His incomprehensible greatness; immense self-knowledge and a deep sense of humility, since I recognize how presumptuous I have been to offend so holy a Father; finally, a great contempt for the things of this earth and an intense love for God and for virtue.

In the past I used to be embarrassed when others came to know what the Lord was doing in me, but for some time past I no longer experience this embarrassment for I see that I am no better on account of these favors, indeed I feel I am worse than before and make poor use of all these graces. As I see myself, I do not know if there are people worse than me; and when I perceive certain things in others which seem to be sin, I cannot convince myself that these people have offended God, even though I see the thing very clearly. The only thing that worries me is evil, which very often distresses me considerably. ... Then I see how full of imperfections I am, and my precious courage seems to abandon me completely. I see myself as extremely weak in the practice of virtue. ... Then I am more than ever convinced that I am good for nothing.[2]

I almost collapse in face of so much loving kindness of the part of the Lord towards this miserable creature; and since I cannot see anything good in myself which could have induced the Lord to act in my soul in this manner, the idea frequently occurs to my mind that perhaps in punishment for my infidelities (which are in fact innumerable, Father!) God is paying me in this life to deprive me of his kingdom, and in this he is perfectly just.[3]

Another time, Padre Pio is giving advice to his spiritual director:

My very dear Father, may the grace of Jesus, our Redeemer, flood your heart more and more and never abandon you, as this is best for your soul! ... With regards to what you ask me, I have nothing to say about your spiritual state except to tell you not to worry and to try more and more to hold firmly to humility and charity which are the main supports of the whole vast building and on which all the rest depends.

Keep firmly on these two virtues, one of which is the lowest, and the other is the highest. The preservation of the whole building depends on the foundation and the roof. If the heart is always striving to practice these two virtues, it will meet with no difficulty in practicing the others.

These are the mothers of virtues and the virtues follow them just as little chicks follow the mother hen.[4]

Padre Agostino is here encouraging Padre Pio about fighting the Devil, who was tormenting him:

Beloved son in Jesus Christ, may Jesus always be yours and may your heart always be the throne of His love! Humility, therefore, humility and always humility. Satan fears and trembles before humble souls. The Lord is willing to do great things, but on condition that we are truly humble.

Attribute everything, then, to Jesus, and may He alone be glorified in you and through you! Please do not worry, therefore, but at the same time continue to live in great humility, fear of God, perfect love for God and your neighbor, blind obedience to authority and to those who direct you in God's name.[5]

12

Isolation and Abandonment

The worst thing that may happen to us is to be rejected, misunderstood, and abandoned. On the cross Jesus experienced the most torturous and excruciating pain — beyond any human imagination — but how much more was that agony enhanced by the rejection and abandonment that came to him from his own apostles and the people who had celebrated his entrance to Jerusalem only days earlier? We humans can endure terrible pain and hardship, but we are crushed when we are rejected.

When you are experiencing that, you are not alone. Jesus went through it and taught us how to prevail against it. Padre Pio went through it and taught us how to make our journey. Job did the same. When Jesus was not welcomed into his hometown, it was painful because he was being rejected by those who knew him all his life. When that happened, the disciples reacted, driven by vengeance and retaliation, "Lord, do you want us to bid fire come down from heaven and consume them?" (Lk 9:54).

Poor Jesus! He had worked so hard to teach and educate his apostles and disciples! It must have been heartbreaking for him to hear what his closest friends, James and John, said about the situation.

Jesus was rejected, and what did he do? He continued his journey, because it's not what people say, but what God says that counts. It is not what the public, or the world want us to be that matters, but what God wants us to be. The Book of Job is an extraordinary example of what a sense of rejection and abandonment can feel like. Do you remember Job's friends who wanted to help him by suggesting that he abandon God? With friends like those, who needs enemies?

For a time Padre Pio, by order of his superiors within the Church, was isolated and punished for no real reason. He was not allowed to see people, to communicate with his spiritual directors, to hear confession, or to celebrate Mass in the church, while ecclesiastical authorities were investigating the stigmata, the spiritual and supernatural phenomena which were present in Padre Pio's life. During this painful period, despite the uproar which had arisen about him, Padre Pio persevered in solitude, prayer, and suffering, always submitting to Church authorities in obedience, and with great confidence in the will of God.

While in isolation, Padre Pio experienced what the Spanish mystic St. John of the Cross called "the dark night of the soul" very intensely. Let us hear what he says:

My very dear Father, may Jesus be always with you, and may He enlighten you as to my interior state at present, of which I am going to tell you. Amen.

I am taking advantage of the brief moments in which I am permitted to withdraw into myself to take stock of my desolate state and to write it down here as best as I can.

For some time, I have been plunged day and night into the dark night of the soul. My spiritual darkness lasts for long hours, long days and frequently for entire weeks.

While I am immersed in this night of the soul, I cannot tell you whether I am in hell or in purgatory. The intervals in which a little light enters my soul are very brief and while I am taking stock of my life, in a flash I fall into this dark prison. Immediately, then, all the favors which the Lord has lavished on my soul are blotted out of my memory. Farewell to the delights with which the Lord had inebriated my soul! Where is that enjoyment of the adorable divine presence? Everything has disappeared from intellect and spirit. It is a continual desert of darkness, dejection, apathy, this is the native land of death, the night of abandonment, the cavern of desolation. Here the soul is far from its God and left to itself. My soul continues to groan beneath the weight of this night by which it is surrounded and penetrated. It is incapable of thinking of supernatural things or even of the simplest matters. And when my soul is just about to grasp a single ray of the divinity, every trace of light immediately disappears.

My will seems to try to love, but in a flash, dear Father, it becomes hard and motionless as a stone. My memory tries to take hold of something to console it, but all in vain.

Isn't this a horrifying state?

But this is not all, my dear Father. What increases my torment more than anything else is the occasional vague remembrance of having previously known and loved this same Lord whom I now feel I neither know nor love, as if He were unknown to me, an absent person, a stranger.

I then try to find at least in creatures the traces of the one for whom my soul longs, but I no longer recognize the usual image of Him who has abandoned me. It is precisely at this point that my soul is overcome by terror and no longer knowing what to do to find its God, it wails bitterly to the Lord: "My God, my God, why have you forsaken me?" [Ps 22:1; see also Mt 27:46; Mk 15:34].

How frightful this is! No one, not even an echo answers in the void that I feel in my soul. But my soul does not yet admit defeat. It makes fresh efforts, but all in vain. Then it feels all warmth die out and its strength come to an end. It recognizes that all sentiments of mercy have disappeared.

Torn away from its Spouse, wounded in its inmost depths, my soul no longer knows what to do in this deepest night; and what increases my torment is the thought that these unbearable sufferings are to last forever, as it seems to me. My poor soul sees no end to this dreadful misery. It appears to me as if a metal wall has shut me into this horrible prison forevermore.

The pains I endure in this state are so many and so acute that I do not see any difference between these and what I would suffer if I were in hell itself. In fact, if I may say so, I suffer even more in this state, due to the love I once had for the Creator. But let me continue.

When this martyrdom has reached its height, it seems to me that my soul seeks consolation in the thought that it must succumb beneath the weight of such sufferings, for it is impossible to endure them any longer.

But praise be to God! The thought that immortality resists even hell itself appears at once to my poor bewildered soul which is about to lose its way. I then realize that my soul still dwells in a living body, and I am about to call out for help, but my cry then seems to suffocate me. At this point I become mute, and I am quite unable to describe to you what then happens within me.

These are quite new experiences and there is no language to describe them. I can only say that this is absolutely the highest peak of suffering and that at that stage

I do not know whether I am pleasing to the Lord or not. For my own part, I am trying to love Him, I want to love Him, but in this night of deepest darkness my blind soul wanders at random, my heart is dried up, my strength is exhausted, and my senses fail me.

I struggle and sigh and weep; I cry out in complaint, but all in vain, until finally my poor soul, crushed by sorrow and with no more strength left, turns to the Lord, and says: "Not my will, O most sweet Jesus, but thine be done."[1]

My very dear Father, may Jesus continue to assist you and may he make you holy!

The furious storm that rages in and around my soul and throws everything into confusion impels me to turn to you before the proper time. More than ever in ignorance of what the future holds for me, startled, and frightened I hurry anxiously to you for some news of Him, some sign of Him and of what I must do to find Him again and be admitted to His embrace, since my present abject state is a horrible one and I am crushed beneath the heavy mass of sufferings and torments.

My situation in the last few days is in fact quite new. I say quite new because I am by no means able to describe it, nor can I find words to penetrate the intensity of certain wanderings of my soul which is more than ever astray, lost, and forsaken.

Father! Dear God! I can utter no other words than these! This is the most refined martyrdom that my frailty could bear. My spirit seems to grow faint every moment beneath the repeated blows of the divine justice, rightly enraged with this wicked creature, and it seems crushed. My heart seems to me to be shattered, for it no longer bleeds from the increasingly ferocious attacks of continual merciless death.

My dear Father! Dear God! I have lost every trace, every vestige of the Supreme Good in the strictest sense of the word. All my frantic searching for this Supreme Good are in vain. I am left alone in my quest, alone in my nothingness and misery, alone with the vivid image of what is possible in experimental knowledge. I am alone, utterly alone, for a strong but quite sterile desire to love this Supreme Bounty.

I see myself obliged to go on living during this total abandonment, when it is desirable to die at every moment as a relief from the agonizing life I am living. Alas! *My God, my God, why have you forsaken me?* I can utter no other cry from the profound bitterness of my heart where I behold myself condemned. Useless were my modest efforts to hold out against this ferocious heat: I am bereft of life; I can no longer hold out. It is urgent that I should live by you and in you and with you, or else I shall die. O life and death! My hour is terrifying, and I do not know, my dear Father, how I can go further, and who knows how much longer this dreadful hour will last.[2]

This long letter continues for two more pages, describing the painful experience of abandonment and of the dark night. However, there is a light at the end of the tunnel, because in Padre Pio's spirituality we find two kinds of abandonment: abandonment by God and abandonment in God. The first being a painful experience, the second being a peaceful experience or, at least, more bearable.

But when, my dear Father, will my exile end? I am sorry about it, but I am resigned to God's will. May the divine plan be accomplished in me if it is for the glory of our dear Jesus. At certain times I suffer deeply in my soul if it were not for the occasional interruption of this torment, who knows what would become of me. Yes, my dear Father, this merciful Lord of ours hastens to my aid when the trial is at its height and like the loving Father He is, He seems to console and encourage me. It is true that I suffer, but I do not complain because Jesus wishes things like this.[3]

In the following letter Padre Pio expresses the importance of the abandonment in God to Padre Agostino. The role has been reversed. Who is really the spiritual director, here, then, Padre Pio or Padre Agostino?

My very dear Father, may the flames of divine love consume within you all that is not Jesus. May the divine Spirit strengthen you by his grace with ever fresh courage so that you may face calmly and tranquilly the war waged by our enemies.

By sacrificing my health, I hasten to answer your most welcome letter, to relieve you of any apprehension which my long silence may have caused.

I sent you a letter last Sunday addressed to San Marco la Catola, but in the uncertainty as to whether you received it or not, I have decided to write this letter, which for reasons already well known to you I take the liberty of sending by means of Raffaelina.

What are you afraid of about your own soul? Don't you know that Jesus is with you and is doing everything within you? Calm yourself, Father, and do not heed those vain and useless fears; fill up the empty places in your heart with ardent love of God. Humble yourself more and more beneath God's powerful hand and always accept cheerfully and humbly the trials He sends us, so that at time of His visitation He may raise us up by His grace. Let us cast all our care upon Him, for He is more concerned about us than a mother for her child. We must keep the eye of faith fixed on Jesus Christ who climbs the hill of Calvary loaded with His cross, and He toils painfully up the steep slope of Golgotha, we should see Him followed by immense throng of souls carrying their own crosses and treading the same path.

Oh, what a beautiful sight this is! Let us fix our mental gaze firmly on it. We see close behind Jesus our most holy Mother, who follows Him perfectly, loaded with her own cross.[4]

13
Poverty

There is no doubt in my mind that the story of the rich man and Lazarus (see Lk 16:19–31) is indeed our story. There is a Lazarus and a rich man in each one of us. There were rich and poor at the time of Jesus, there were rich and poor at the time of Padre Pio, there are rich and poor today, and there will be rich and poor forever. The interesting point Jesus wants to make is not how much the rich had, and Lazarus did not have. Rather, he emphasizes the great gap between the haves and have-nots, the abyss between good and bad, between the desire to be good and the fear to make a commitment to do so. This great abyss is not out there, somewhere; it is within us, right here.

When we can experience this dichotomy, then, we experience happiness. The striking point in the story of the rich man and Lazarus is that the rich man did not directly do anything to harm Lazarus. The rich man never abused Lazarus; he did not chase him away from his palace or from the gate; he did not beat the poor sick beggar; he did not report him to the police for trespassing or to the health inspector for not being clean or wearing clean clothes. Why, then, did the rich man receive such a harsh sentence? Not because he was rich, not at all! Being rich can be a blessing to help others. The rich man was condemned to hell because he simply didn't care, he never even noticed Lazarus, so he did nothing.

Poverty can be a state of mind, and a state of being, just as truly as it is a state of living. Padre Pio could have been the richest person on earth, for the huge number of people who gave generous donations for the beautiful projects initiated by Pio. But the humble friar did not have a penny, as anyone who has seen his room would attest. Humility and charity were the foundation that sustained the true poverty of Padre Pio. Chapter 4 of our Capuchin constitutions speaks about our life in poverty, based on the Gospels: "The gospel ideal of poverty led Francis to humility of heart, to radical disposition of self, to compassion for the poor and the weak, and to share their life."[1]

Padre Pio was very much aware of this, so he was unhappy if friars did not live the poverty of St. Francis, our founder. The poverty of Padre Pio was so complete that he owned not even his breviary (prayer book):

Jesus has complained a lot about that phenomenon[2] ... by which the holy vow of poverty has been violated even in our own Province, which he looks upon with special benevolence in preference to others.

There have been expenses, travel, transfers, etc., which were not strictly necessary. Let us place ourselves in the Lord's hands so that this may not happen again.

Someone has stolen my breviary. What am I to do? Punish me if you wish, my dear Father, but please provide me with one as soon as possible.[3]

I hope you will pardon what I am about to say and not accuse me of shameful arrogance. Jesus complains a great deal about men's ingratitude, but especially of the ingratitude of our own mother Province. Oh, my dear Father, how often is Jesus offended by our own friars! "The religious," says Jesus, "consider themselves so many princes. Look, isn't it only princes who indulge in correspondence by telegram, and with great parsimony? Aren't religious today doing the very same? Where is their vow of poverty? How many souls are scandalized by this violation of their profession! My Father will no longer tolerate them. I too would like to abandon them, but alas! (Here Jesus stops and weeps, then continues) My heart is made of love. Speak my son, speak; let them hear how angry I am ..."

Now, dear Father, to whom can I turn if not to you who by prudence, wisdom, and authority, can do so much to alleviate Jesus' suffering? Set to work, my dear Father, and be watchful. Jesus will help you. Consider, moreover, the great responsibility that rests on you.[4]

My very dear Father, I am committing to writing what I should have liked to tell you by word of mouth. You will forgive my liberty I am taking.

I draw your attention to some considerable expenses that it is intended to incur for this Friary, and which do not seem to bear the stamp of real necessity.

There is talk of putting new floor in the entire building, not excluding the cloister. I doubt if it is worthwhile sinking tens and tens of thousands of lire to improve a house belonging to others[5] and to give the place an appearance, or undoubtedly, contrary to our simplicity and seraphic poverty.

I am not referring to what has already been done (I mean to speak all the time of expenses for repairs or for damage done) and you yourself will have been able to see some defects but let us look further ahead."[6]

Padre Pio, very much aware of his strict poverty, asked some poignant questions to Padre Benedetto in the following letter:

Now I want to ask you for some clarifications. ... If one of us religious is offered money by a person in the world with the express request to use it as he thinks best in conscience, for his own greater good, for God's glory and for the relief of his neighbor, is it contrary to our rule for the religious who receives this offering on the above terms to use it as he thinks best in all conscience?

Is it lawful for us to recommend to generous and rich people those who are in need so that they may be relieved in their poverty? Is it lawful for us to do this if a person comes to us and gives us an offering for the express purpose of helping poor people? Please answer me on these points.[7]

Padre Benedetto, in fact, does answer:

Here are the replies to your questions: 1. It is more than lawful to recommend the poor, especially the hidden poor, to those who are rich and generous.

2. It is lawful to distribute to the poor the offerings received for this purpose, because in so doing one is merely carrying out the will of the donors and by no means exercising power.

3. It would be blameworthy to receive money when the donors have not in any way indicated the purpose; but when they state the use to be made of it, even imprecisely, then there is no offense against a duty, because we are using it within the range of their desires.

Let us not forget the poor nuns who are suffering and hungry.[8]

14
Listening Prayer

It was said that St. Francis of Assisi was not praying, he was the prayer. When I lived with Padre Pio, I noticed that he had the busiest schedule that anybody could handle and yet he was able to pray and to pray constantly. This reminds me of how foolish we are when we say: "I wish I had time to pray!" The truth is that you make the time, the time doesn't make you. The busier we are, the more we need to pray.

The most important aspect of any prayer is "attentive listening." When Jesus made important statements, he always said, "Pay attention to what I am telling you." If we miss this first step in our prayer, we miss the whole prayer. "Listen" is the first word of the Rule of Saint Benedict, who tells us to, in our prayer, attend to the Lord "with the ear of the heart."

Padre Pio was very much aware of this way of "listening prayer." If you saw him any time during the day, he often seemed like he was in another world. We learn from Padre Pio's prayer of listening that God takes the initiative. The *Catechism of the Catholic Church* tells us that, "In prayer, the faithful God's initiative of love always comes first; our own first step is always a response."[1] As when the phone rings: Someone has taken the initiative to call; you pick up the receiver and the conversation begins.

Now let us listen to Padre Pio on this subject:

How great is my misfortune, my dear Father! Who can understand it? I understand I am a mystery to myself. I cannot understand myself.

You tell me that the venerable Sister Thérèse of the Child Jesus used to say: I do not want to choose either to die or to live but let Jesus do as he likes with me! I see clearly that this is the image of all souls who are stripped of self and fulfilled with God. But how far my own soul is from this denudation! I am unable to check the impulses of my heart, yet I am trying, Father, to comply with what the Venerable Sister Thérèse has said, which ought to be said by every soul inflamed with love of God.

To my embarrassment, though, I must admit that I fail when it is a question of remaining a prisoner in the body of death. This is a sign, I say, that there is no love for God in me, for if there were, since the spirit which vivifies is the same, the effect should also be the same.

To put more clearly: if the one who acts in me were the same one who acted in Sister Thérèse, the sentiment of this holy soul would also be verified in me. Now, tell me, am I not right in doubting this? Alas! who will set me free from such cruel torment of the heart?

I accept, O my God, all the torments of this earth bunched together. I desire them as my portion, but I could never resign myself to being separated from you for lack of love. Ah, for pity's sake, do not permit this poor soul to go astray; never allow my hope to be deluded; never let me be separated from you; and if I am at this moment, unknowingly, separated from you, then rescue me this very moment. Enlighten my mind, O my God, so that I may know myself fully and recognize the great love you have shown me and allow me to enjoy for all eternity the supreme beauty of your divine countenance.

O dear Jesus, never let me lose the precious treasure that you are for me. My Lord and my God, I experience too vividly in my soul the ineffable tenderness that pours forth from your eyes, the love with which you, my only Good, condescend to gaze on this miserable creature.

How can the torment of my heart be placated, the agony of knowing I am far from you? My soul is aware of the terrible battle I endured when you, O my Beloved, hid yourself from me! O most tender Lover how clearly is this terrible and frightening image imprinted on my soul!

Who will ever be capable of eliminating or extinguishing the ardent flames of this fire which burns in my breast for you? Ah, Lord, do not take pleasure in hiding yourself; you know what confusion and tumult this causes in all the faculties of my soul and in all my feelings! You see that my soul cannot bear the cruel torment of this abandonment, for you have enchanted it too much O infinite Beauty!

You know how anxiously my soul seeks you. This anxiety is no less than that of your spouse in the sacred Songs: my soul too, like that holy spouse, wanders in the public streets and in the squares and adjures the daughters of Jerusalem, if you find my beloved, that you tell him I am sick with love (see Song 5:8).

In this state, how well my soul understands what is written in the Psalms: My spirit fainted: my soul yearns for your saving help (see Ps 119:81).[2]

Perhaps you may have noticed how well Padre Pio blends the teaching of the Doctor of the Church, St. Thérèse of the Child Jesus, the Gospel, and the Old Testament. The listening prayer, for Padre Pio, was not only listening to God speaking to his heart and mind, but also listening to the word of God, which is something like the Lectio Divina in our modern time.

15
Diabolical Attacks

We can certainly say that Padre Pio was not a friend of the Devil and vice versa. They fought tooth and nail to overcome each other. The strategy of Padre Pio was prayer and reliance upon God's help; the strategy of the Devil was to tempt, to deceive with false promises, and, at times, to hurt Padre Pio physically and spiritually.

We learn from Padre Pio's letters that the attacks of the Devil were skillfully planned to hurt Padre Pio on two fronts: externally by beating him and keeping him away from his routine ministry to the faithful and encouraging him not to write to his spiritual directors; internally, the Devil's attacks were directed toward demolishing his will and intellect and preventing him from practicing the theological virtues.

By the way, Padre Pio did not use the word *devil* all the time, but he used humoristic names to designate the Devil. Also, it should be noted that, sometimes, Pio had to struggle with more than one devil. He would mockingly refer to a "devil" or "devils" as "big whiskers," "whiskers," "the ogre," "scoundrel," "miserable, evil spirit," "wretch," "filthy wretch," "foul beast," "woeful wretch," "hideous faces," "impure spirits," "those scoundrels," "wicked spirit," "horrible beast," "accursed beast," "infamous apostate," "impure apostates," "gallows-bird," "howling wild beasts," "malignant deceiver," and "prince of darkness."

Once, a friar, Padre Giacomo Piccirillo, who was taking care of Padre Pio in the early sixties, told me that he heard Padre Pio calling the Devil *Barbablu* (Bluebeard), but he did not know why. My presumption is that perhaps Padre Pio knew the 1697

fairy tale of Charles Perrault which showed Bluebeard as an ux-
oricide and a serial killer, therefore an evil person.

Now, let us read what Padre Pio had to say about diabolical
attacks:

> My very dear Father, who will set me free from the mis-
> eries in which I am placed? The temptations, especially,
> pursue me more relentlessly than ever. They are a source
> of great suffering, not because of the continual violence
> I must do myself, but because they are so repellent and
> persistently hostile and in view of my great fear of of-
> fending God from one moment to the next, for there are
> moments at which I am right on the brink of the preci-
> pice and about to fall. Even during my hours of rest the
> devil does not cease to torment my soul in various ways.
>
> It is true that I have been strong up to the present
> and by God's grace have not yielded to the enemy's wiles,
> but who knows what may happen to me in the future?
> I should indeed be glad if Jesus would grant me a brief
> respite. But may His will be done in my regard!
>
> Even from far away do not fail to invoke maledic-
> tions on this common enemy of ours, so that he may
> leave me in peace. I ask you in charity to pray to the
> Lord for me just as I have done and will continue to do
> for you, not that He may take me out of the world before
> it pleases Him to do so, but that He may keep me from
> evil.[1]
>
> The spiritual war has not ceased, and, in fact, it is
> fiercer than ever. To put it briefly, dear Father, the enemy
> of our salvation is so furious that he hardly leaves me
> a moment's peace and wages war on me in a variety of
> ways. I desire the grace from Jesus to be set free from
> this, because I fear to offend Him. If He wants to mortify

me, I wish He would do so by corporal suffering, which I would willingly accept.[2]

Moreover, during the last few days the devil has been up to all sorts of mischief, and he is doing everything he possibly can to me. The "wretch" will redouble his efforts to harm me. But I fear nothing except offense against God. It seems to me that the "wretch" is more annoyed with you than with me, for he wants to deprive me of your direction. In fact, I must make a great effort to tell you about my affairs. Intense pain in the head almost prevents me from seeing where to place my pen.[3]

The attacks become more frequent and more intense with the passing of time.

My very dear Father, I must tell you what has happened to me during the past two nights.

I had a very bad time the night before last; from about ten o'clock, when I went to bed, until five o'clock in the morning, that "wretch" did nothing but beat me continuously. He presented to my mind many diabolical suggestions, thoughts of despair, distrust in God. But praise be to Jesus, for I defended myself by saying to Him repeatedly: "your wounds are my merit."

I really thought that was the last night of my life, or that if I did not die, I should lose my reason. But may Jesus be blessed, for nothing of the sort occurred.

At five in the morning, when that "wretch" left me, my whole body became so cold that I trembled from head to foot like a reed exposed to a violent wind. This lasted a couple of hours. I spat blood.[4]

The one who is always by my side has come at last to rout the enemy so that I can write you these few lines.

But I am very weak. The enemy hardly ever leaves me alone, and he beats me continually. He is trying to poison my life with his infernal snares.

He is greatly annoyed that I should tell you this. He is suggesting to me to stop telling you what goes on between himself and me, and he hints that I should tell you about the good visits, as these, he says, are the only ones which can please and edify you. ... When the Archpriest became aware of the attacks of those "impure apostates" with reference to your letters, he advised me to go to him on receipt of your next letter so as to open it in his presence.

This I did on receiving your last. But when we opened it, we found it completely covered with ink stains. Was this also a vendetta on the part of the "ogre"? I cannot believe that you would have sent it to me like that, aware as you are of the weakness of my sight.

At first the writing seemed illegible to us, but after we had placed the letter on the crucifix it became a little clearer, although we could only read it with great difficulty. This letter has been kept carefully.[5]

About this letter, here is the declaration of the Archpriest, Salvatore Pannullo: "When the letter had been placed on the crucifix, sprinkled with holy water, and the holy exorcism had been pronounced over it, it was possible to read it as at present. I called my niece, Grazia Pannullo, a teacher, who read it in the presence of myself and Padre Pio, unaware of what had been done before I called her. In faith, etc. ... Pietrelcina, August 25, 1919. Signed, The Archpriest, Salvatore Pannullo."

The satanic attacks continue:

To the trial of spiritual fears and trembling, with an

occasional spice of desolation, Jesus is adding the long and varied trial of the physical suffering, making use of those ugly "wretches" for the purpose.

Listen to what I had to endure a few evenings ago from those "impure apostates." The night was already well advanced when they began their attack with a devilish din, and although I saw nothing in the beginning, I understood who was making that strange noise. Instead of being frightened, I got ready to fight them with scornful smile on my lips. Then they appeared to me in the most abominable forms and to make me act dishonorably they began to present themselves to me all dressed up.

But thank heaven, I scolded them soundly and treated them as they deserve. Then, when they saw all their efforts going up in smoke, they hurled themselves on me, threw me to the ground, and proceeded to beat me very severely, throwing pillows, books, and chairs around the room, with desperate shrieks and most obscene language. Fortunately, the rooms nearby and beneath my own are unoccupied.[6]

My dear Father, is it true that I am in Jesus' arms, that He is mine and I am entirely His? This is unfortunately the question which comes to my lips frequently and spontaneously.

When I received your letter recently and before I had opened it, those "wretches" told me to tear it up or else throw it in the fire. If I did this, they would withdraw for good and would never trouble me again.

I kept silent without giving them any answer, while in my heart I despised them. Then they added: "We want this merely as a condition for our withdrawal. In doing so you will not be showing contempt for anyone." I replied that nothing would make me change my mind.

They flung themselves upon me like so many hungry tigers, cursing me and threatening to make me pay for it. My dear Father, they kept their word! From that day onward they have beaten me every day. But I am not frightened."[7]

And the battle goes on:

My dear Father, I am very happy just now. Jesus never stops loving me despite all my shortcomings, for He allows these ugly-faced creatures to afflict me incessantly. For the past twenty-two days Jesus has allowed them to vent their anger on me continually, my body, dear Father, is bruised all over, from all the blows it has received at the hands of our enemies.

More than once they even went so far as to pull off my nightshirt and beat me in that state. Tell me, now, was it not Jesus who helped me in those awful moments when I was bereft of all other assistance and the devils tried to destroy me body and soul? Add to this that even when they withdrew, I remained stripped for quite a long time as I was powerless to move, and this in the present severely cold season.[8]

Those "wretches" have not stopped beating me. Sometimes they throw me out of bed, and they have gone so far as to strip me and beat me in that state. But I am no longer afraid of them. Jesus is always most loving in His treatment of me and at times He has even lifted me from the floor and put me back in bed.[9]

16
Temptations

This topic is as old as the creation of the world, as recorded in the Book of Genesis. Every human being has experienced temptations; we have experienced temptations since we were born, and they will be with us until we die.

Temptations always involve promises and illusions. When we are tempted, we are given a promise that looks very good, or usually comes disguised as something good. The Devil made all kinds of promises to Jesus if only Jesus would do certain things. The promises appealed to what we humans would call good things — food, power, glory. Jesus rejected all of them because he understood, as we sometimes do not, that they were empty promises, only but illusions.

Temptations may come in different shapes or forms. Sometimes it may be somebody quoting the Bible to you. We learn from the Gospel of Luke that the Devil used this technique skillfully, but without success. There is no doubt that Satan knows the Bible very well. However, Jesus counteracts with the same technique — quoting the Bible and dispelling Satan's illusions. At times, we may not be wise and strong as Jesus was, we may not know Holy Scripture as intimately as Jesus did, to counteract Satan's deceptions, but we are assured by God that our temptations are never stronger than we are, that temptations do not control us, we control them.

Let us look at Luke's account of the temptations (see Lk 4:1–13). Firstly, the Devil sets up the stage: He thinks to take advantage of Jesus in the desert, and he knows that Jesus needs food to survive, power to lead, and all glory for the Father. So naturally, the evil one sets about tempting Jesus with food, power, and glory.

Secondly, the Devil uses a very common technique of tempting human pride with the teasing doubt of the word *if*. He says, "If you are the son of God …" If you are? You are not sure? Temptations often begin with an "if" and if we start rationalizing the "if," we will probably know defeat. Children use this technique constantly: "If you think you are so fast, then …" Salesmen use it frequently, as well: "If you need a comfortable sofa, this is the one you really need, and, fortunately, it is on sale."

Here is a pragmatic way to handle temptations:

First, don't panic. The Devil loves to make you fearful and insecure as he promises happiness. He can make hell out of heaven.

Several years ago, a Texas newspaper ran an account of an automobile accident which included the following: "Passers-by carried the unconscious driver to a nearby service station. The crash victim, as he opened his eyes, panicked, struggling mightily to break away from the circle of good Samaritans gathered around him. Whereupon a rescue team arrived, quickly subdued him, and took him to a hospital. Asked later why he had made that desperate attempt to get away from his rescuers, he explained that they had taken him to a Shell station … and someone was standing in front of the 'S' … so he thought he was in hell." Sometimes, we make more noise than the Devil himself.

Temptations and sufferings are integral parts of our lives, as are success and joy. From the Gospel of Luke, we learn that there is victory in suffering. Happiness does not just happen; we assist its manifestation in our lives by disposition and openness. Dissect the word *happiness* and you get "happens in us." In the engineering field, we say, if it does not work, redesign it until it works. Additionally, we can "kiss" our difficulties and temptations in order to become victorious over them. Let me explain:

A priest was having dinner at a parishioner's home. After dinner he was challenged to play a video game by the seven-year-old boy. Unfortunately, the priest kept on losing as he tried to figure out the intricacies of the game. After a bad mistake, the youngster said to the pastor: "Father, remember the KISS principle." The frustrated priest asked, "The what, now?"

The youngster replied: "Keep It Simple, Silly."

To love Jesus and to overcome temptations is not complicated at all: Let us use this KISS method. Keep your eyes and your heart focused on Jesus.

By the way, sometimes the Devil does not really tempt us; we can manufacture our temptations. How often do we buy a package of cookies that we know we shouldn't want, and that will only call to us from the cabinet?

After some general reflections about temptations, let us see if Padre Pio's temptations have something in common with Jesus' temptations and ours. I cannot speak for him; let him speak about it. In reading his letters, I have noticed a great attempt by Pio "not to give in." We learn from his life that temptations and sufferings can be worthwhile, because they make us strong. It seems to me that the goal of the Devil was to break Padre Pio down and to destroy his relationship with God. Pio had to endure terrible and strong challenges against faith, hope, and love. I do not wish to impose my point of view as I read "between the lines" in Padre Pio's letters, but I leave it up to you. Perhaps you will see this topic from a different perspective.

The saint faces the Devil's threats with determination and courage:

> My heart is brimming over with happiness, and I feel more and more prepared to meet any suffering which may come, as long as it is a matter of pleasing Jesus.
>
> It is also true, though, that the devil cannot refrain

from his efforts to make me lose my peace of soul and lessen the great confidence I have in the divine mercy. He tries to do this chiefly by means of continual temptations against holy purity which he arouses in my imagination, at times even when I merely glance at things which I do not call holy, but which are perhaps indifferent.

I laugh at all this as being of no account, following your advice. It sometimes worries me, though, that I am not quite sure if I have been ready to put up a fight at the enemy's very first attack. Undoubtedly when I examine my conscience at present, I should prefer to die rather than deliberately offend my dear Jesus by a single sin however small.[1]

I have no means of thanking our dear Jesus who gives me such strength and courage to bear not only the many ailments He sends me, but even the continual temptations which He in fact permits and which grow numerous day by day. These temptations make me tremble from head to foot with the fear of offending God. I hope that in the future as in the past I may not fall victim to them.[2]

Dear Father, the devil continues to make war on me and unfortunately shows no sign of admitting defeat. … Later, when I prayed at the feet of Jesus, I seemed to feel no trace of the burden entailed in trying to overcome myself when tempted, or of the chagrin occasioned by my troubles.

The temptations regarding my life in the world are those which trouble my heart most and obscure my mind, bringing on a cold sweat and, I was about to say, making me tremble from head to foot.[3]

My dear Father, if it were not for the war which the

devil wages against me continually, I should be in paradise, but I am in the hands of the devil, who is trying to snatch me from the arms of Jesus. Dear God! What a war he is waging against me! There are moments in which I am on the point of losing my reason through the continual violence I must do myself. How many tears and groans, dear Father, I send up to heaven to be set free. But no matter, I will never tire of praying to Jesus. It is true that my prayers deserve punishment rather than reward, for I have offended Jesus only too often by my innumerable sins.[4]

Padre Gerardo Di Flumeri, who edited Padre Pio's letters, has an interesting running commentary on the expression "my innumerable sins." He says that this is pious exaggeration often found in Catholic biography; it has its origin in the deep inner awareness which the soul acquires of human weakness and the holiness of God. "These and other similar expressions were denied with authority by Padre Benedetto who wrote: 'There never were, nor are there, serious or slight sins in your soul and what you appear to see is a mere semblance or representation. This is the whole truth of the matter.'"[5]

There is no doubt that the temptations were used by Padre Pio for the greater good and with unlimited confidence that God will never allow the Devil to test us beyond our strength, as it is clearly outlined by St. Paul: "God is faithful, and he will not let you be tempted beyond your strength, but with the temptation will also provide the way of escape, that you may be also able to endure it" (1 Cor 10:13).

As the temptations continue without mercy, the purification of suffering takes place, even though Padre Pio may not be aware of the inner process which is going on.

My dear Father, I am hardly capable of telling you all that has been happening to me during the past few days, for even as I write, the devil is waging war on me more than ever. I am unable to repulse the attacks which the enemy of salvation is making on me.

Who will set me free, dear Father, from all these temptations and afflictions? Who is to console me? Who will give me strength to hold out as I should? Who would believe that a person is tormented even during his hours of rest? Well then, my dear Father, I can assure you that even these hours are a time of exceeding torment for me. I only find a little respite by thinking over and reading your instructions. But these are only fleeting moments, because the enemy is watchful all the time and starts all over again. In comparison with my bodily sufferings, the spiritual struggles are much greater, although my physical sufferings are also increasing continually.

I wish, dear Father, that I could have, I do not say a long respite, but at least an hour each day. But let the most holy and most lovable will of God be done in me and all around me, always and in all things! This is what has enabled me to carry on.

The devil wants me for himself at all costs. With all I am suffering; if I were less Christian, I should certainly believe myself possessed. I do not know why it is that God has not been moved to pity for me to set me free. I only know that He never acts except for most holy ends which are for our good.

Now tell me, Father, for the love of Jesus and of our beautiful Sorrowful Virgin, if I have something in my heart even very small which is not pleasing to God, for with your help I want to pluck it out at all costs. Perhaps this permission is a punishment for the offenses of which I may still be guilty and unless I first get rid of these, He will not be moved to compassion. ... Always if this is for the greater glory of His divine majesty and for the good of my soul.[6]

Meanwhile the devil is taking advantage of my physical weakness and of my impossibility to act, to torment me more with images and phantoms. My dear Father, what is God's purpose in allowing the devil so much freedom? Despair is trying to take hold of me, yet believe me, Father, I have no intention of displeasing God. I cannot account for and much less understand how it can ever be possible that such a resolute will prepared to do good can be combined with all these human miseries.[7]

After the physical attacks, the Devil, who never declared defeat, attacked Padre Pio on a spiritual level. The Devil was able to beat and torture Padre Pio's body, but he failed in his strategy because Padre Pio faced the Devil head on and, we might say, while losing the battles but winning the war. So, the strategy of the Devil changes dynamics, which we might describe as him saying, "I am not done with you yet; I will move from external assaults to internal or spiritual assaults, which are going to be merciless and will make you miserable. Stay tuned ... the best (worst) is yet to come!"

The combat with hell has reached the point at which it is no longer possible for me to continue. The ship of my soul is about to be overwhelmed by the ocean waves.

My dear Father, I just cannot go on any longer; I feel the ground giving way beneath my feet and my strength is failing. I am about to die, and I taste every kind of death at each moment of my life. The battle is extremely fierce, and I feel I must succumb from one moment to the next. The waters of tribulation are about to overcome me, and I am on the point of drowning. The fighting is heavy on both sides. When I measure the opposing forces, I am terrified by the enemy ranks. I feel crushed by the infernal forces, and I am afraid of being reduced to nothingness from one minute to the next.

The enemy is very strong, and all things considered it seems that victory must smile on him. Alas! Who is to save me from the hands of so strong and powerful an enemy who allows me not a moment's freedom, day or night?

Is it possible that the Lord will allow my downfall? Unhappily, this is what I deserve, but can it be that the heavenly Father's goodness will be outdone by my wickedness? This will never, never be, my dear Father. I feel again the love of my God rising like a giant in my poor heart and I still have the confidence and strength to cry aloud with St. Peter: Lord, save me, I am perishing![8]

The enemies are continually rising, Father, against the ship and they cry out in unison: "Let us knock him down, let us crush him, since he is weak and cannot hold out much longer."

Alas, my Father, who will set me free from these roaring lions all ready to devour me? You say only too well that while the Lord is testing us by His crosses and sufferings, He always leaves in our hearts a glimmer of light by which we continue to have great trust in Him and to see His immense goodness.[9]

My weakness makes me tremble and break out in cold perspiration. Satan with his malignant wiles never tires of waging war on me and attacking my little citadel, besieging it on all sides. In a word, Satan is for me like a powerful foe who, when he resolves to capture a fortress is not intent to attack one wall or one rampart, but surrounds it entirely, attacks and torments it on every side.

My dear Father, the malignant wiles of Satan strike terror into my heart, but from God alone through Jesus Christ I hope for the grace to obtain the victory continually and never to be defeated. ... To your question as to when the scourge will end, I give no answer, except to say that I am utterly in the dark about it. The Lord has shut himself up in a complete mutism.[10]

Faith has been badly shaken by the constant attacks of the Devil, and Pio is experiencing the "dark night" even more intensely than usual. The road which once was full of light is now shrouded in fog or total darkness. Padre Pio asks Padre Agostino to come to his rescue:

Dear God! Those wicked spirits, dear Father, are making every effort to destroy me. They want to defeat me at all costs. They seem to take advantage precisely of my bodily weakness to vent their rage upon me more fully, to see if in this state they cannot snatch from my breast the faith and fortitude that come to me from the Father of all light.

At certain moments I see myself on the brink of the precipice and then it seems to me that the tide of battle is about to turn in favor of those scoundrels. I feel myself trembling all over. A mortal agony invades my wretched soul and overflows into my poor body. My limbs appear to me to be paralyzed. Then it seems to me as if my life had stopped, as if it were suspended.

This is a sad and mournful spectacle: only one who

undergoes this trial can imagine it. It is a very harsh trial, my dear Father, which exposes to the extreme risk of offending our Savior and Redeemer! Here, indeed, one risks all for all. Will the merciful Lord continue to show me His mercy by giving me the strength and perseverance, which He has bestowed on me so far, that I may invariably defeat and overcome this enemy of ours who is so strong and powerful?

I hope for all things through your prayers and those of others, and with the help of the Spirit of Jesus Christ. I confess, my dear Father, that in all these battles, although I am so weak that it seems I must succumb from one moment to the next, I feel certain, nevertheless, that according to my expectation and hope I shall never be confounded and that Jesus Christ, as is invariably the case, will now be glorified in my soul and in my body which will suffer no damage whatsoever.[11]

An infinite number of fears assails me at every moment. Temptations against faith which would drive me to deny everything. My dear Father, how hard it is to believe! May the Lord help me and not allow me to cast the shadow of doubt on what He has been pleased to reveal to us. I ask for death as a relief from my torments. May the Lord grant it to me without delay, for I just cannot go on any longer. ... My hand is trembling, and I am unable to hold the pen. I am shaken with sobs which rob me of speech.[12]

There are times, moreover, when I am assailed by violent temptations against faith. I am certain that my will does not yield, but my imagination is so inflamed and presents the temptation in such a bright color that sin seems not merely something indifferent but even delightful.

This gives rise to all those dejected thoughts, to diffidence and thoughts of despair and — please do not be horrified, Father — even blasphemous thoughts. I am terrified in face of such a combat, I tremble and do violence to myself, and I am certain that by God's grace I do not fall.[13]

Once again, these days my soul has gone down into hell, once again the Lord has exposed me to Satan's fury. His attacks are violent and continual. This infamous apostate wants to wrench from my heart what is holiest in it: my faith.

I feel my will firmly attached to God, but I must also admit that my physical and moral strength are growing increasingly weaker, due to the extreme combat in which I am engaged. Has the Lord perhaps granted the prayer I addressed to Him with great insistence when I was in Naples, when I asked Him to replace this trial by another, even harder one? If this were the case, dear Father, there would be reason to be consoled.[14]

Later, Padre Pio expressed deep concern:

The struggle against faith is raging with increasing intensity.[15]

My soul is continually enveloped in darkness which is becoming deeper as time goes on. The temptations against faith are increasing all the time. I am therefore living in constant darkness, trying to see, but all in vain.

Dear God! When shall I see — I do not say the sun — but at least the dawn? The only thing that sustains me is the word of those in authority. May God's will be done?![16]

17

Obedience

Here is how the Capuchin Constitutions of 2013 describe the vow of obedience:

> Following in the foot prints of the Lord Jesus, who throughout His life "placed His will in the will of the Father," the brothers offer their wills by the profession of obedience as a sacrifice of themselves to God, conform themselves continually to the saving will of God, whom they love above all else, and bind themselves to the service of the Church.
>
> Moreover, by living in obedience, together with the brotherhood they discover the will of God with greater confidence, manifest the communion of the three Divine Persons, and strengthen brotherly union itself. In the same spirit of generosity with which they promised to observe the gospel counsels, let them obey the superiors with faith and love for God's will, in an active and responsible way. May they be fully aware that the freely made offering of their own will to God contributes enormously to their personal perfection and becomes for others a witness of the kingdom of God. "Clinging to Christ, who although He was Son learned obedience through his sufferings," let them accept the limitations of the human instruments through whom the will of God is mediated. Remembering that the cross is the proof of the greatest love calling for the gift of self, let them persevere in brotherly communion, and in this

way live in perfect obedience and share in the work of redemption. (2, 165)

If obedience is sometimes difficult in the religious life, it was almost heroic in Padre Pio's life. He obeyed the Church and the superiors unconditionally, despite trials, persecutions, punishments, isolation, and misunderstandings.

> What am I to say about myself? I am a mystery to myself and if I succeed in carrying on it is because the good God has reserved the final and surest word for authority on this earth and because there is no better rule than the will and the desire of the Superior. I confide in this authority as a baby in its mother's arms and I hope and trust in God that I will not go astray, although my feelings would have me believe anything to be possible. ... The Provincial remains adamant regarding that matter of which you know. ... May the divine will be done! I desire nothing else.[1]
>
> From the moral point of view, in my own opinion I am getting worse and worse, although authority tells me and declares the opposite.
>
> To tell the truth, the only thing that enables me to keep my balance is authority. I am suffering resignedly, and I anxiously await the dawn; I do not expect the return of the sun which has been promised to me for a long time, but which never appears. I repeat that I await the dawn, because my weak sight could not bear the brilliance of the sun."[2]
>
> The storm of which I spoke to you when we met is raging more fiercely than ever. My faith in authority is not lacking and the efforts I make to abide by it increase the pains caused by those thorns which are piercing my heart.[3]

I am ready to believe invariably what authority tells me and to follow its advice, although this brings me no comfort whatsoever.[4]

I merely cry out and from this you will understand the extent of my poverty and lowliness, my misery and indigence. Implore help for me from heaven; perfect conformity with the divine and holy designs although these are concealed from me; resolute, constant, and unshaken docility where obedience is concerned, which is my one support in the raging storm, the only raft to which I can cling in this spiritual shipwreck.

I renounce all will and knowledge of my own, all satisfaction and information and I declare myself the utterly obedient son of my spiritual guide in this punishment from the Most High. What more is there? Much more, dear God! I ask you for the strength to suffer stripped of all consolation. Make these resolutions of mine constant, steadfast and fruitful, so that they may at least suffice to disarm your fury.

Offer them yourself, my Supreme Good, to your offended Majesty, but not before you have strengthened them by your divine power, while I will endeavor to find a resting-place in my unbearable affliction on this bed of sharp and cruel thorns and will receive from your hands the capacity to relish as my food this rejection and abandonment you mete out to me. … My God! This cry is necessary, my dear Father, and it is all that is left to me during such affliction. I understand nothing anymore. I greatly fear to be abandoned forever to myself and in this fear, I clutch or try to clutch at obedience, but even this seems to elude me.[5]

I see clearly that I hardly have the strength to continue the struggle. I am dying of hunger before a richly laden table; I am parched with thirst beneath the fountain from which pure water is gushing. What more? The light blinds me before it dispels the fog around me. How is this? I am tired of wearying my guide. Support and obedience itself merely serve as props to prevent me from abandoning myself to utter abandonment.[6]

18
Call to Holiness

The universal call to holiness has its origin in the Bible. Just to quote one of the many phrases used in the Scriptures, St. Paul, writing to the people of Ephesus says: "There is one body and one Spirit, just as you were called to the one hope that belongs to your call" (Eph 4:4). In more recent time (1930), Pope Pius XI, in his encyclical on Christian marriage, *Casti Connubii*, reiterates the same universal call to holiness: "For all men of every condition, in whatever honorable walk of life they may be, can and ought to imitate that most perfect example of holiness placed before man by God, namely Christ Our Lord, and by God's grace to arrive at the summit of perfection."[1]

Furthermore, the universal call to holiness is a particularly special emphasis of the Second Vatican Council, where we read in *Lumen Gentium*:

> The Church, whose mystery is set forth by this Sacred Synod, is believed to be indefectibly holy. Indeed Christ, the Son of God, who with the Father and the Spirit is praised as "uniquely holy," loved the Church as His bride, delivering himself up for her. He did this that He might sanctify her [Eph 5:25–26]. He joined her to himself as His own body and brought it to perfection by the gift of the Holy Spirit for God's glory. Therefore in the Church, everyone whether belonging to the hierarchy, or being cared for by it, is called to holiness, according to the saying of the Apostle: "For this is the will of God, your sanctification" [1 Thes 4:3; see also Eph 1:4]. How-

ever, this holiness of the Church is unceasingly manifested, and must be manifested, in the fruits of grace
which the Spirit produces in the faithful; it is expressed
in many ways in individuals, who in their walk of life,
tend toward the perfection of charity, thus causing the
edification of others; in a very special way this (holiness) appears in the practice of the counsels, custom-
arily called "evangelical." This practice of the counsels,
under the impulsion of the Holy Spirit, undertaken by
many Christians, either privately or in a Church-ap-
proved condition or state of life, gives and must give in
the world an outstanding witness and example of this
same holiness. (No. 39)

Some important points about the universal vocation of all Christians may be broken down from that paragraph. The fathers of
the Second Vatican Council see the call to holiness as deriving
from two sources: the mystery of the Church and, more funda-
mentally, the mystery of Christ himself.

The Church is believed to be "unfailingly holy," for Christ
gave himself up for her "to sanctify her," uniting her to himself
as his Body and perfecting her by the gift of the Holy Spirit. Because the Church is holy, all members of the Church are called to
be holy — to become what they are — and to manifest this holiness in their lives by faithfulness to the movement of the Spirit,
by the practice of charity.

Christ himself preached holiness of life to all. "Be perfect,
as your heavenly Father is perfect" (Mt 5:48). He provided the
means for holiness, sending the Spirit who pours love into our
hearts, that we might love God above all, and love each other as
Christ loves us. Moreover, in baptism the faithful put on Christ,
becoming sons and daughters of God and sharers in the divine
nature. Thus, we are made holy by the grace of God. We must

then hold on to this holiness and live it out in our concrete lives. We must live in a manner that befits holiness.

The council concludes then that all members of the Church, all Christ's faithful, whatever their rank or status, are called to the fullness of Christian life and the perfection of charity.

Padre Pio was very much aware of this universal call to holiness from an early age. That is why he entered the Capuchin order and became a priest. But in addition to this universal call to holiness, he perceived in his youth that God had a special mission for him, and that his mission, like all of us, was to be united with the suffering of humanity and to be co-redeemers with Christ.

VOCATION

The vocation to co-redemption is emphasized by Padre Pio's spiritual director:

> My dear Piuccio: No, you have not been abandoned, you are not the object of God's vengeful justice, there is no unworthiness.
>
> All that is happening to you is the effect of love. It is a trial, it is a vocation to co-redemption, and hence a source of glory. Given this as certain and undoubted fact, all anxiety and trepidation created by the enemy from the wicked delight he takes in tormenting you and permitted by the Supreme Good for the purpose already mentioned — all such anxiety disappears.
>
> To call yourself a thorn that torments the lovable Lord and to recognize your unworthiness as a clear and obvious fact which leaves no room for even the shadow of the opposite, is a downright lie, a scene presented to you in vivid and glowing colors by the skillful artist of darkness whose treachery is equal to his ability to en-

hance his picture by the bold use of light and shade. It is untrue that you have corresponded badly with grace and by your unfaithfulness cut yourself off from God, earning the refusal of His embrace and His irreconcilable enmity. The Lord is with you! He is with you: patient, suffering, eager love, crushed and trampled upon, heartbroken; in the shadows of the night and even more so in the desolation of Gethsemane, he is associated with your suffering and associates you with His own.

This is the whole of the matter; this is the truth and the only truth. Yours is not a purgation but a painful union.

The fact of the wound completes your passion just as it completed the Passion of the Beloved on the cross. Will the light of happiness of resurrection arrive? I hope so if he is pleased that it should.[2]

Only seven years earlier, Pio wrote:

Meanwhile, what am I to do to correspond to such great mercy? How am I ever to repay him for such great benefits? If you only knew how many times in the past, I have exchanged Jesus for some contemptible thing appertaining to this world! I see something mysterious in myself: I am constantly sorry for the sins I have committed. I resolve continually never to commit them again, yet, I must admit with bitter tears, that despite all this I am still very imperfect, and it seems to me that I very often offend the Lord. At times I am really in despair because it seems to me almost impossible that Jesus should let me go astray. Oh, what on earth is all this? Explain it to me a little. However, all this happens to me without my perceiving it, for I have by no means the will to offend

God even to the slightest extent.

I also suffer greatly, Father, when I see how people ignore Jesus, and what is worse, how they even insult Him, especially by those dreadful blasphemies. I should like to die, or at least become deaf rather than hear so many insults offered to God by men.

I have prayed to the Lord as follows: Lord, let me die rather than be present when people are offending you! Please recommend me to the Lord and ask Him for this grace for men if it should be for his greater glory.[3]

Padre Pio's mission as co-redeemer becomes more challenging as time goes by. He does not really understand what is going on; He says: "I am a mystery to myself." How are God's designs implemented in Padre Pio's life?

But long live Jesus, for even when He persecutes me, He does not allow my soul to succumb to despair. I believe at the apex of my soul alone, although without the slightest consolation and without seeing, because of your assurances and assertions.

To put it briefly: My belief is a great effort of my poor will, against all human reasoning on my part. Perhaps it is for this reason that I will never be able to receive any solace either at the sensory level or in the higher part of my soul.

In fact, my belief is the result of continual attempts to overcome myself. This, my dear Father, is not a matter of several times a day, but is continual, and if I were to act differently, I could not help becoming unfaithful to my God.

The night is growing even darker, and I do not know what the Lord has in store for me.

There are so many things that I would like to tell you, Father, but I am unable to do so. I realize that I am a mystery to myself.

When will the moment come when the fog will be dispelled in my soul? When will the sun rise within me? Am I to hope for it in this world? I no longer believe this can happen.[4]

In November 1922, alluding to his entry into the Capuchin order, Padre Pio wrote the following words to one of his spiritual daughters: "Infinite praise and thanks be to you, O my God, you hid me away from the eyes of all, but already at that time you had entrusted a very great mission to your son. A mission that is known to you and me alone ... O God! Show yourself more and more to this poor heart of mine and complete in me the work you have begun. I hear deep within me a voice which says to me repeatedly: sanctify yourself and make others holy."[5]

COLLABORATION

The process continues: From being called to a redemptive mission to being a collaborator of the same redemptive mission, Padre Pio clearly understood that his mission included carrying and embracing the cross, therefore accepting the martyrdom he had to endure in his lifetime:

In the past, my desire to see God used to make me conform to His will, considering myself as I did to be in exile, and conformity helped me to endure this life, but now, dear Father, this is no longer within my power. My reason, oppressed by the pain of seeing myself still in exile, comes to the point where it is no longer its own master and can only consider the motives it has for tormenting me.

I experience such a strange solitude that neither any creature here below nor those who dwell in heaven, even though my Beloved is there, could keep me company. I find no relief in this world, where everything wearies and torments me. Yet I want to suffer all this torture for my whole life, if this is pleasing to God, even though I know as well as I know myself that this means agony for my soul.

On other occasions, although I am not thinking of such a thing at all, my soul goes on fire with the keenest desire to possess Jesus entirely. Then, with an indescribable vividness communicated to my soul by the Lord, I am shown as in a mirror my whole future life as nothing but a martyrdom. Without knowing why, and with unspeakable love, I yearn for death. Despite all my efforts I am driven to ask God with tears in my eyes to let me be taken from this exile. I feel inflamed with such a lively and ardent desire to please God and I am gripped by such a fear of falling into any slightest imperfection that I would like to flee from all dealings with creatures. Simultaneously, however, another desire rises like a giant in my heart, the longing to be in the midst of all peoples to proclaim at the top of my voice who this great God of mercy is.

Now and then, apart from these simultaneously painful and delightful feelings, the Lord grants me certain pleasures that even [I] myself do not understand. The happiness I experience is so extreme that I would like to share it with others so that they might help me to thank the Lord. Again, when I am busy about even indifferent things, a mere word about God or the sudden thought of some such word affects me so deeply that I am carried out of myself. Then the Lord usually grants

me the grace of revealing to me some secrets which remain indelibly impressed on my soul. I am unable, however, to describe all these secrets, for often, I have no
adequate words for the purpose. Even the secrets which
I succeed to some extent in putting into words, lose so
much of their splendor that I regard myself with compassion and disgust.

As a result of these favors which sometimes last for
several days, my will remains enraptured, and my intellect completely absorbed in what it has beheld. But when
I come to myself completely, I am filled with embarrassment, seeing how unworthy I am of such favors. I would
like to have an infinite number of lives to spend entirely
for God and it is at this point that I complain loudly to
Jesus that He offers me so few occasions to suffer.

A holy and learned person, whom I consulted about
these things has eased my mind and assured me that
there is no deception here.[6]

As Padre Pio continues his journey of co-redemption, he experiences setbacks, uncertainties, fears, discouragement; however, he
is convinced to have been called to go through this journey, and
therefore, he accepts all the above as long as he can participate in
carrying Jesus' cross.

He chooses souls and despite my unworthiness, He has
chosen mine also to help him in the tremendous task
of men's salvation. The more these souls suffer without
the slightest consolation, the more the sufferings of our
good Jesus are alleviated.

This is the whole reason I desire to suffer more and
more without the slightest consolation. In this consists
of all my joy. Unfortunately, I need courage, but Jesus

will not refuse anything. I can testify to this from long experience, if we do not stop asking Him for what we need.

Now and again, even from a distance, continue to curse our common enemy. Let your heart fly towards me, just as mine goes very often to you. But do not forget that I am an egoist where suffering is concerned. I want to suffer alone and while I am impatient to depart and go to Jesus, I should reproach myself if I were to seek to be deprived of the cross even for a single hour, or worse still, if others were to step in and rob me of it.

All I want you to do is to ask our most sweet Jesus insistently to keep me far from sin.[7]

The Lord then consoles me and causes me to exult "in my weakness" [see 2 Cor 12:9].

Believe me, dear Father, I find happiness in my afflictions, Jesus himself wants these sufferings from me, as He needs them for souls. But I ask myself what relief I can give Him by my suffering! What a destiny! Oh, to what heights has our most sweet Jesus raised my soul!

I am glad to have to manifest all the gratuitous favors which Jesus has bestowed on my soul. But it gives me food for thought when I consider that God stoops down to beg sufferings from such a wretched creature. Tell me, my dear Father, is his purity not sullied by this heart of mine which has for a long time harbored so much iniquity. ...

Again, at night when I close my eyes, the veil is lifted and I see paradise open before me; and gladdened by this vision I sleep with a smile of sweet beatitude on my lips and a perfectly tranquil countenance, waiting for the little companion of my childhood to come to waken me, so that we may sing together the morning praises to the Beloved of our hearts.

Oh, my dear Father, if the knowledge of my state arouses in you even a single thought other than compassion, I beg of you to direct it to my Beloved on my behalf in token of my appreciation and gratitude.[8]

It seems that there is a prediction of his stigmata, when Jesus says: "You will feel the suffering in your soul, but more acutely in your body."

During these days which are so solemn for me since they are feasts of the heavenly Child, I have frequently been seized by those excesses of divine love which cause my poor heart to grow quite faint.

Completely penetrated By Jesus' condescension towards me, I addressed my usual prayer to him with greater confidence: "Oh, Jesus, if I could only love you, if I could only suffer as much as I should like in order to make you happy and make some kind of reparation for men's ingratitude towards you!"

But Jesus made His voice more clearly audible in my heart: "My son, love is recognized in suffering; you will feel it acutely in your soul and even more acutely in your body."

My dear Father, to me these words remain very obscure. Those "wretches" are trying to torment me in every way; I complain to Jesus of this, and I hear Him say to me: "Courage! After the battle comes peace." He tells me I must be faithful and courageous. I am ready for anything if I am doing His will. Only pray, I implore you, that the little bit of life I have left may be spent for His glory and that I may make use of this time in such a way as to spread the light.[9]

Who could resist Him? I realize that I have made Him suffer exceedingly by my failings, that I have made Him weep too much by my ingratitude, that I have offended Him too grievously. I want nobody but Jesus, I desire nothing else (which is Jesus' own desire) than His sufferings. Allow me to say it, since no one can hear us, I am ready even to be deprived forever of the tenderness which Jesus lavishes on me, I am prepared to bear His hiding His beautiful eyes from me if He does not hide from me His love, for this would cause me death. But I could not bear to be deprived of sufferings, I lack the strength for this. Perhaps, I have not yet expressed myself adequately about the secret of this suffering. Jesus, the Man of Sorrows, wants all Christians to imitate Him. Now, Jesus has offered this chalice to me also; I have accepted it, and this is why He does not spare me. My poor sufferings are of no value, yet Jesus is pleased to accept them, because He loved suffering very much while He was on earth. Hence, on certain special days on which His sufferings were greater on this earth, He makes me experience this suffering more severely. Now, would this alone not suffice to humiliate me and make me try to remain hidden from the eyes of men, since I have been made worthy to suffer with Jesus and like Jesus?"[10]

Very much aware of his call to collaborate with Jesus's sufferings, Padre Pio is also convinced that his journey can only be the ascent of Golgotha.

But, alas, after a while I came to myself and felt my whole life weighing heavily on my shoulders. I feel crushed beneath the weight of the long exile which remains before me. It is true that just one more step … and the cross will be set up on Golgotha, but you must agree that the step to be taken to set up the cross will require further time, and to agonize there with Jesus will take time.

May the Lord be pleased to present to my mind this day which must dawn as less long than it seems to me. I feel an extreme need to tell you about the present state of my soul, a new state of which I dread to be obliged to speak. For the present I just cannot speak of it, due to the state of my health, but I hope to do so before long. Would you believe, dear Father, that it has taken me four days to write this letter?[11]

I remind you that I belong with great ardor to everyone and for this reason I am suffering immensely for all.[12]

I am ready for anything as long as Jesus is happy and will save the souls of my brothers, especially those He has entrusted to my care.[13]

IMPLEMENTATION
Vocation and collaboration in co-redemption lead us into implementation of Jesus' mission on earth, that is "being a victim" of this free offering to God with painful and challenging consequences. As early as 1910, Padre Pio asked permission to be a victim from his spiritual director, Padre Benedetto.

I want to ask your permission for something. For some time, I have felt the need to offer myself to the Lord as a victim for poor sinners and for the souls in Purgatory. This desire has been growing continually in my heart so that it has now become what I would call a strong passion. I have in fact made this offering to the Lord several times, beseeching Him to pour out upon me the punishments prepared for sinners and for the souls in a state of purgation, even increasing them a hundred-fold for me, if He converts and saves sinners and quickly admits to paradise the souls of Purgatory, but I should now like to make this offering to the Lord in obedience to you. It seems to me that Jesus really wants this. I am sure that you will have no difficulty in granting me this permission.[14]

Did I not tell you that Jesus wants me to suffer without any consolation? Has He not asked me and chosen me to be one of His victims? Our most sweet Jesus has really made me understand the full significance of being a victim. It is necessary, dear Father, to reach the "*Consummatum est*" (It is finished) and "*In manus tuas*" (into your hands).[15]

Jesus, His beloved Mother, the little Angel and the others continue to encourage me, and they keep on repeating that a victim properly so-called must lose all His blood. To have such a tender father by one's side in the battle is sweet and consoling.[16]

What am I to say of myself? My soul must endure a continual combat. I see no other way out than to abandon myself in the arms of Jesus where He often allows me to fall asleep. Blessed sleep! Happy refreshment for the soul in the struggle it endures.[17]

Listen, my dear Father, to the justified complaints of our most sweet Jesus: "With what ingratitude is my love for them repaid! I should be less offended by them if I had loved them less. My Father does not want to stop loving them. But ... (and here Jesus paused, sighed, then continued) but, alas! My heart is made to love! Weak and cowardly men make no effort to overcome temptation and indeed they take delight in their wickedness.

The souls for whom I have a special predilection fail me when put to the test, the weak give way to discouragement and despair, while the strong are relaxing by degrees.

They leave me alone by night, alone by day in the churches. They no longer care about the Sacrament of the altar. Hardly anyone ever speaks of this Sacrament of love, and even those who do, alas, with great indifference and coldness.

My heart is forgotten. Nobody thinks any more of my love and I am continually grieved. For many people, my house has become an amusement center. Even my ministers, whom I have loved as the apple of my eye, who ought to console my heart brimming over with sorrow, who ought to assist me in the redemption of souls — who would believe it? — even by my ministers I must be treated with ingratitude and slighted. I behold, my son (here he remained silent, sobs contracted his throat and he wept secretly) many people who act hypocritically and betray me by sacrilegious communions, trampling underfoot the light and strength which I give them continually. …

Jesus continues to complain. Dear Father, how bad I feel when I see Jesus' weeping! Have you experienced this too? "My son," Jesus went on, "I need victims to calm my Father's just divine anger; renew the sacrifice of your whole self and do so without any reserve."

I have renewed the sacrifice of my life, dear Father, and if I experience some feeling of sadness, it is in the contemplation of the God of Sorrows.[18]

By being a victim in the process of co-redemption, as Padre Pio was, some surprises would take place, without prior notice:

"While this was taking place, I had time to offer myself entirely to the Lord for the same intention which the Holy Father had when he recommended to the whole Church to offer prayers and sacrifices. I hardly finished doing so when I felt myself falling into this most harsh prison and heard the loud clang of the prison door as it closed behind me. Cruel shackles seemed to close on me and bind me tightly in hell without even an instant's respite."[19]

19
Mystical Phenomena

Any experience of true mystical phenomena always includes the following:

- An intuition of God, as distinct from discursive knowledge, with profound penetration into divine mysteries
- An experimental or quasi-experimental knowledge of God. This is the essential phenomenon of the mystical life and is usually accompanied by spiritual joy, interior absorption in God, disdain for worldly pleasures, and a desire for greater perfection
- Passive purification of the senses, which presupposes the active purgation of senses and spirit
- Continued awareness of the presence of God, accompanied by "sleep" or suspension of the faculties, filial fear of God, love of suffering, divine touches, spiritual sensations, flights of the spirit leading to ecstasy, wounds of love, and interior communications
- Passive purgation of the spirit
- Total death to self, heroism in the practice of virtue, joy in persecution, zeal for the salvation of souls, and relative confirmation of grace

To be the subject of mystical phenomena, one must be a contemplative. Of course, each person is both contemplative and active, and so it was with Padre Pio as is clearly demonstrated in his work as a tireless confessor and army chaplain, while constantly engaged in prayer, contemplation, and reliving the mystery of the cross on the altar of sacrifice.

The question is this: What percentage of action and contemplation was present in Pio's life on earth? When we read the Gospel stories of Mary, "the contemplative" sister and Martha "the active" one, we may get some clues to help assess Padre Pio's commingling of action and contemplation.

It would be an exercise in futility to determine how much of "Mary or Martha" is in each person because a constant dynamism is present within each of us and the two dimensions are constantly in a variable process of being and becoming.

Considering all the events and circumstances of Padre Pio's life, I tend to believe that a high percentage of his journey was contemplation rather than action, even though he would spend about nine hours daily in hearing confessions; however, even his confessional ministry became partially contemplation because he was doing it for the glory of God and salvation of souls.

I agree with Padre Gerardo Di Flumeri, the editor of his letters, that "the mystical phenomena accompany this phase of the contemplative life or life of union, and which are found in his letters.[1] The same editor of Padre Pio's letters has a comprehensive explanation of the mystical phenomena of Padre Pio, emerging from his letters. Here is the synopsis of his introduction to the *Letters*: "First, Impulses of love; then, Mystical touches, followed by strokes and wounds of love (Stigmatization), with the grace of transverberation."[2]

IMPULSES OF LOVE
Let us hear from Padre Pio:

> I do not know whether Father Provincial let you read my last letter to him. If he did, you will have been able

to get a faint idea of what the Lord is doing within me at present.

I feel my heart and my inmost being completely absorbed by the mounting flames of an immense fire. These flames cause my poor soul to give vent to pitiful laments. Yet who would believe it? While my soul experiences an atrocious agony caused by the flames I have described, it is filled at the same time with an exceeding sweetness which calls forth immense love of God.

I feel myself annihilated, dear Father, and I cannot find anywhere to hide from the gift of the divine Master. I am sick with an illness of the heart. I cannot go on any longer. The thread of life seems ready to break from one moment to the next, yet this moment never comes.

My dear Father, the soul is in a sad state when God has made it sick with His love. For pity's sake, ask the Lord to end my days, for I just haven't the strength to continue in this state. I see no other remedy for my heart's sickness than to be consumed once and for all by these flames which burn without consuming me.

Do not think that it is the soul alone that suffers this agony. The body too, although indirectly, has a share in it to an enormous extent. Since this divine action has begun within me, my body is becoming utterly powerless.

Speak to me about all this and tell me how I should act. I see myself more and more loaded with debts in the sight of the divine Majesty, and I do not see how I can pay them. So many and so utterly sublime are His graces that my soul feels crushed beneath them.[3]

This light, in fact, has never grown, but you will have to agree that it is precisely this light which causes the soul greater pain than can be humanly conceived. It shows up the divine goodness as something the soul cannot enjoy by loving possession, something it can only long for from afar with painful yearnings to possess it. This light makes the soul yearn for God, the source of all good, and often the pain of its desire is revealed by abundant tears.

My dear Father, while my soul continues in this state, everything is a torment. The poor thing is continually held in a most agonizing contemplation in which God gives marvelous knowledge of himself and by showing himself far off, causes my soul such acute pain as to reduce it to mortal agony.

Do not imagine that the body has no part in these atrocious sufferings experienced by my soul. No, it participates in a very surprising way that is quite unknown to the children of suffering.

Father, when will there be an end to the agony I am enduring in soul and body as a result of the painful wounding which has taken place and which continues? Dear God! I can no longer go on, my dear Father, I feel I am dying a thousand deaths at every instant. I feel myself being consumed by a mysterious force, a deep and penetrating force which keeps me continually in a delightful but most painful languor.

What on earth is this? Is it a sin to complain to God of such harshness? And if it is a sin, how am I to suffocate these laments when an irresistible force drives me to complain to our sweet Lord, a force over which I have absolutely no control?[4]

MYSTICAL TOUCHES

During the experience of "impulses of love," Padre Pio knew acute pain counterbalanced by ineffable sweetness. His soul yearned to be united forever with God.

This stage of the "mystical touches" became more sophisticated with more detailed signs and symbols, which included a fusion of hearts, a substantial touch, and a kiss of love. Let Padre Pio speak about it:

> But our good Jesus, who permitted the "ogre" to treat me in this fashion, did not fail to console me afterwards and to strengthen me in spirit.
>
> I was hardly able to get to the divine Prisoner to say Mass. When Mass was over, I remained with Jesus in thanksgiving. Oh, how sweet was the colloquy with paradise that morning! It was such that, although I want to tell you all about it, I cannot. There were things which cannot be translated into human language without losing their deep and heavenly meaning. The heart of Jesus and my own — allow me to use the expression — were fused. No longer were two hearts beating but only one. My own heart had disappeared, as a drop of water is lost in the ocean. Jesus was its paradise, its king. My joy was so intense and deep that I could bear no more, and tears of happiness poured down my cheeks.
>
> Yes, dear Father, man cannot understand that when paradise is poured into a heart, this afflicted, exiled, weak and mortal heart cannot bear it without weeping. I repeat it was the joy that filled my heart which caused me to weep for so long.
>
> This visit, believe me, restored me completely. Praise be to the divine Prisoner![5]
>
> Father, may I be allowed to express myself freely at least to you: I am crucified by love! I can no longer go on. This is too delicate food for one accustomed to coarse fare and it is for this reason that it continually causes me extreme spiritual indigestion to the point at

which my poor soul cries out in acute pain and love at the same time. My wretched soul cannot adapt to this new manner of the Lord's dealings with it. Thus, the kiss and the touch, which I would describe as substantial, that this most loving heavenly Father imprints on my soul, still cause me extreme suffering.

May our good Jesus enlighten you as to my real state! Meanwhile I implore you to do me the further charity of telling me what you think about this.

My dear Father, the fact of having to attend to the necessities of life such as eating, drinking, sleeping, etc. is so burdensome to me that I can find no comparison unless in the pains which our martyrs must have suffered in their supreme trial.

Do not think, Father, that there is any exaggeration in this comparison because, in fact, it is exactly how things are. If the Lord in his goodness did not prevent me from reflecting while I am performing these actions, as has happened in the past, I know I could not continue for very long, for I feel the ground giving way beneath my feet. May the Lord assist me and free me from this great torment. May He behave towards me and treat me as I ought to be treated. I constantly rebel against the divine action, and I certainly do not deserve to be treated in this way.[6]

Only once did I feel in the deepest recesses of my spirit something so delicate that I do not know how to explain it to you. First, without seeing anything, my soul became aware of His presence and then, as I would describe it, he came so close to my soul that I felt His touch. To give you a feeble image of it, it was like what happens when your body feels the pressure of another body against it.

I do not know how to describe it otherwise. I merely confess that I was seized with the greatest fear in the beginning and that by degrees this fear became a heavenly rapture. It seemed to me that I was no longer in the state of a traveler, and I cannot tell you whether at that moment I was still aware of being in this body of mine. Only God knows this, and I am unable to tell you anything further to give you a better idea of this event.[7]

Here is what happened to me on that day [the feast of Corpus Christi]. During my Mass in the morning I was touched by a living breath. I cannot convey the slightest idea of what happened within me in that fleeting moment. I felt completely shaken, filled with extreme terror and almost passed away. This was followed by a state of total calm such as I had never experienced.

This terror, agitation and calm in quick succession were not caused by the sight of anything but something which I felt touching me in the deepest recesses of my soul. I am unable to say any more about this occurrence. May God be pleased to make you understand what really happened to me.[8]

STROKES AND WOUNDS OF LOVE

Some strokes and wounds are spiritual and interior, some are external and visible. Let us begin with interior strokes of love.

Let Padre Pio describe these:

Listen now, to what happened to me last Friday. I was in the church making my thanksgiving after Mass, when I suddenly felt my heart wounded by a fiery dart, so sharp and ardent that I thought I should die.

I have no suitable words to convey to you the intensity of this flame. I am quite powerless to describe it.

Do you believe it? The soul which is the victim of such consolations becomes dumb. It seemed to me as if an invisible power were plunging my whole being into fire. Dear God! What fire! What delight!

I have experienced a great many of the transports of love, and for some time have remained, as it were, outside this world. On the other occasions, however, this fire was less intense, whereas this time another moment, another second, and my soul would have been separated from my body and would have gone to Jesus.

Oh, what a wonderful thing it is to become a victim of divine love! But at present, how is my soul? My dear Father, Jesus has now withdrawn His fiery dart, but I am mortally wounded.[9]

Yes, dear Father — and I am telling you the truth — my anguish is so great that I doubt if it will be any greater at the supreme hour of my death. It is as if all my bones were being destroyed. Although I do not see this with my bodily eyes, but very clearly with those of my soul. I feel I am being stabbed time after time with a sharp-pointed knife which seems to emit fire. This blade pierces my heart and penetrates even my entrails, then it is swiftly withdrawn and after a few moments the action is repeated.

All this, as the knife-thrusts are multiplied, causes an immense love of God to blaze with increasing intensity in my soul.

The pain caused by this wound which He inflicts on me and the sweetness which accompanies it are so intense that I cannot even begin to describe them.

However, dear Father, this pain and this sweetness are completely spiritual, although it is also true that they are shared by the body to a high degree.

If the Lord of goodness has allowed you to experience this, you will understand to the full what I have told you is true.[10]

Eight months later, Padre Pio wrote about the same topic:

All my thoughts tell me that I am far from God and no healing balsam can soothe this cruel wound. No medicine is of any use, nor is there any consolation apart from that of suffering a veritable martyrdom for so worthy a cause.

My dear Father, who among mortal men can imagine the harshness of the trial to which I am subjected? Who can guess the depth of the wound which has been opened in my heart? Who can identify the hand that launched the arrows? Who can indicate the remedy to alleviate such cruel torment?

Alas, how stupid I am, my dear Father! If it were possible to treat me with the miserable remedies of human art, this would certainly cease to be a pain from such a high sphere.

Meanwhile, how am I to live while confined to this harsh prison? It is not true that man's life is short here below; no, his life is too long, it is endless. What reason is there for me to remain any longer imprisoned in this world? For me there is no balsam capable of soothing this cruel wound except to resign myself to pleasing my most tender Lord in this also.

Ah, dear Father, let us pray together to the most tender Comforter of all true lovers in these same words: "O my God, delightful repose of those who love you, grant at last this rest to a heart enamored of Your beauty, to a heart that lives for one purpose alone, for You alone will and can reduce the torment of a soul that is wasting away from the desire to be united with you forever.[11]

WOUNDS OF LOVE

These are connected to the interior strokes of love, but they are deeper and longer lasting. The effect of this mystical stage is *transverberation*, which is piercing of the heart physically, and *stigmatization*, which is the appearance of wounds in some parts of the body such as the hands, feet, and side, something first experienced by St. Francis of Assisi.

Transverberation

This phenomenon is also called "the Seraph's assault." St. John of the Cross tells us that "the soul inflamed with love of God is interiorly attacked by a Seraph, who sets it on fire by piercing it through with a fiery dart." We know that St. Teresa of Jesus had this experience, and so did Padre Pio on August 5, 1918, when he described the event to Padre Benedetto:

> For this reason [obedience], I am led to manifest to you what happened to me on the evening of the 5th of this month and all day on the 6th.
>
> I am quite unable to convey to you what occurred during this period of utter torment. While I was hearing the boys' confessions on the evening of the 5th, I was suddenly terrorized by the sight of a celestial person who presented himself to my mind's eye. He had in his hand a sort of weapon like a very long sharp-pointed steel blade which seemed to emit fire. At the very instant that I saw all this, I saw that person hurl the weapon into my soul with all his might. I cried out with difficulty and felt I was dying. I asked the boy to leave because I felt ill and no longer had the strength to continue.

This agony lasted uninterruptedly until the morning of the 7th. I cannot tell you how much I suffered during this period of anguish, even my entrails were torn and ruptured by the weapon, and nothing was spared. From that day on I have been mortally wounded. I feel in the depths of my soul a wound that is always open, and which causes me continual agony.

Is this not a new punishment inflicted upon me by divine justice? Judge for yourself how much truth there is in this, and whether I have not every reason to be afraid and to suffer extreme anguish.[12]

Padre Benedetto answered:

"What you are experiencing is a vocation to co-redemption ... and the fact of the wound completes your passion just as it completed the Passion of the Beloved on the cross."[13]

The phenomenon of transverberation is not over yet:

I see myself submerged in an ocean of fire! The wound which has been reopened bleeds incessantly. This alone is enough to make me die a thousand times. Dear God, why don't I die? Oh, do You not see that life itself is a torment for this soul You have wounded? You are even cruel when You turn a deaf ear to my cries and do not comfort me! But what am I saying? Forgive me, Father, I am beside myself and do not know what I am saying. The excessive pain of this open wound makes me angry against my will, drives me crazy and makes me delirious. I am powerless in face of it.[14]

For several days I have been aware of something like

a steel blade which extends in an oblique line from the lower part of my heart to just below my right shoulder. It causes me extreme pain and never allows me to rest. What can this be? I began to be aware of this phenomenon after a further apparition of the usual mysterious person of 5 and 6 of August and 20 of October[15] of whom I told you, if you remember, in previous letters.[16]

An intense scrutiny by doctors and experts in the field of medicine and psychology followed the stage of transverberation and before the stigmatization, but the conclusions were always the same: "We do not understand; it's something supernatural." We do have a statement of a Capuchin Friar, Padre Paolino of Casacalenda, who witnessed this phenomenon:

As an item of interest, I must say that what struck me most at the sight of the wounds was the shape of the wound in the side, which is to be seen on the same side as the heart and not on the other side as I heard from a number of people. It is almost the shape of an "X," from which it can be deduced that there are two wounds, and this fits in with the fact I have heard mentioned but cannot prove for lack of reliable documents, that is, that long before the stigmata, Padre Pio received a swordthrust through the heart from an angel. The other thing that impressed me was that this wound has the appearance of a severe burn, and that it is not superficial but got deep into the side.[17]

Stigmatization
In the mystical field, stigmatization is an extension of the wound of love or an outward sign and projection of the wound within the soul. The first symptoms were disclosed by Padre Pio himself:

Yesterday evening, something happened to me which I can neither explain nor understand. In the center of the palms of my hands a red patch appeared, about the size of a cent and accompanied by acute pain. The pain was much more acute in the left hand, and it persists. I also feel some pain in the soles of my feet.

The phenomenon has been repeated several times for almost a year now, but for some time past it had not occurred. Do not be disturbed by the fact that this is the first time I have mentioned it, for it was invariably overcome by abominable shame. If you only knew what it costs me to tell you about it now![18]

From Thursday evening until Saturday and on Tuesday, there is a painful tragedy for me. My heart, hands and feet seem to be pierced through by a sword. I feel great pain on this account.[19]

This process from the invisible signs (transverberation) to the visible signs (stigmatization) takes place in such a way that only Padre Pio can give more details on this extraordinary and supernatural event:

What can I tell you in answer to your questions regarding my crucifixion? My God! What embarrassment and humiliation I suffer by being obliged to explain what You have done to this wretched creature!

On the morning of the 20th of last month, in the choir, after I had celebrated Mass, I yielded to a drowsiness like a sweet sleep. All the internal and external senses and even the very faculties of my soul were immersed in indescribable stillness. Absolute silence surrounded and invaded me. I was suddenly filled with great peace and abandonment which effaced everything else and caused a lull in the turmoil. All this happened in a flash.

While this was taking place, I saw before me a mysterious person similar to the one I had seen on the evening of August 5. The only difference was that his hands and feet and side were dripping blood. This sight terrified me and what I felt at that moment is indescribable. I thought I should die and really should have died if the Lord had not intervened and strengthened my heart, which was about to burst out of my chest.

The vision disappeared and I became aware that my hands, feet, and side were dripping blood. Imagine the agony I experienced and continue to experience almost every day.

The heart wound bleeds continually, especially from Thursday evening until Saturday. Dear Father, I am dying of pain because of the wounds and the resulting embarrassment I feel deep in my soul. I am afraid I shall bleed to death if the Lord does not hear my heartfelt supplication to relieve me from this condition. Will Jesus, who is so good, grant me this grace? Will He at least free me from the embarrassment caused by these outward signs? I will raise my voice and will not stop imploring Him until, in His mercy, He takes away, not the wound or the pain, which is impossible since I wish to be inebriated with pain, but these outward signs which cause me embarrassment and unbearable humiliation."[20]

Padre Pio celebrating the Eucharist

Part 2
Spiritual Guidance

"The Lord be with you"

20
From Directee to Director

Why would a holy man such as Padre Pio need spiritual guidance if he is a role model for many people who wish to be better believers and lovers of God? The editor of Padre Pio's letters has a good answer: "As a genuine master of the spiritual life, Padre Pio had very clear ideas on the importance of spiritual direction for progress toward perfection."[1] In November 1946, Padre Giovanni da Baggio, OFM Cap., spent a little time in San Giovanni Rotondo and had an opportunity for long conversations with Padre Pio on various topics. In an account of one of these conversations, he says: "I asked him if one can do without a spiritual director. He replied that the confessor can suffice and that when he is not able to understand certain spiritual situations, then we must confide in God's goodness. However, he said, acting on your own is like studying by yourself; with a teacher, you get on much more quickly and better."[2]

Padre Pio chose Padre Benedetto, who was Provincial Minister, and Padre Agostino "the professor," and followed their advice and spiritual guidance as a good student or disciple would do. Both spiritual directors later requested the saint to be their teacher and director in matters of spirituality. Padre Pio considered the request unusual and absurd — that the disciple should become the teacher and vice versa, or as he put it, "that the patient should write prescriptions and administer medicines to his doctor."[3] Pio did, finally, consent to direct both spiritually.

However, if you wish to see the art of spiritual guidance, you must read Padre Pio's letters to his spiritual daughters. Because of the variety of subjects, themes, and topics, it would be impossible to be analytical or to attempt to cover the whole spectrum of Pio's spiritual direction. I will try to follow the three basic principles outlined in the introduction to the third volume of his letters.[4]

DUC IN ALTUM (GO HIGHER)

The universal call to holiness is a basic formula for any spiritual direction. This is what Padre Pio wrote to Erminia Gargani: "This, my dearest daughter, is the constant wish of him who ardently desires to see you ascend to the very highest of Christian perfection,"[5] and to Maria Gargani: "To ask to make us holy is neither presumption nor audacity, because it is the same as desiring to love Him greatly."[6]

On the contrary, he wrote to Erminia Gargani: "It is an excellent thing to aspire to extreme perfection in the Christian life. But it is not necessary to philosophize except on one's emendations and progress in daily events, leaving the result of your desires to God's providence."[7]

There is never hesitancy in Padre Pio's letters in focusing on the universal call to holiness and the need to "go higher." Let me quote some openings from his letters:

- May the grace of the Lord be always with you and make you holy.
- May the Infant Jesus comfort you and make you holy.
- May Jesus always be in the midst of your hearts and make you holy.
- And may he make you holy.
- May he make you worthy of his divine embraces.
- May he render you worthy of his divine charisms.
- May he make you always more worthy of ascent to greater heights.
- May he transform us all into seraphim of love.

- May he grant you the fullness of Christian perfection.
- ... to perfect transformation in him.
- May he transform you in heavenly charity.

However, the call to holiness and the ascent to greater heights, requires total self-denial and filial abandonment:

Abandon yourself in His paternal arms like a child who, to grow, eats what the father prepares every day, hoping he will not let him go without food in proportion to his appetite and needs. ... Do not doubt my prayers, which are certainly poor, but still assiduous for you. I have never ceased, nor will I cease to pray to the most sweet God that He may be pleased to accomplish His holy work in you; that is, that you may have a strong desire and intention to reach perfection in the Christian life; a desire which you must love and nurture tenderly in your heart, as the work of the Holy Spirit, and a spark of His divine fire.

In Rome, I saw a tree which is said to have been planted by the Patriarch, Saint Dominic. All the faithful, going to see it, caressed it, out of love for him who planted it. And for this reason, I, having seen in you the tree of desire for sanctity which God planted in your soul, love it tenderly and feel pleasure when I consider it. Therefore, O my good daughter, I exhort you too, to do the same, and to say along with me: "May God see to it that you grow to be a faithful tree, divine heavenly seed. May God see to it that you produce mature fruit, and when you have done so, may God preserve you from the wind that makes the fruit fall to the ground, where indiscreet beasts devour it."

My most beloved daughter, this desire must be within you just like the orange trees of the Genoa Riviera, which are laden w ith fruit, flowers and leaves combined, almost all year long, so that your desires may always bear fruit when the occasion presents itself, working a little every day. Nonetheless, you must never cease to desire objects and means by which to make further progress.[8]

In the process of responding to God's call to holiness and to reach the summit of perfection, Padre Pio warned us that to accomplish the precept of loving God, we must keep in mind the golden rule, which is not that of loving God as he deserves, but to the degree weak and human nature is capable of. In fact, this point was clearly underlined when he wrote:

You complain and doubt your love of Jesus. But tell me, whoever was it that told you, you do not love our most sweet Savior? Ah, I know, you would like to love God as He deserves. But you know also that all this is not possible for us creatures. God commands us to love Him not as much as He deserves, because He knows our limitations and therefore doesn't ask us to do what we cannot, but rather, He commands us to love Him in accordance with our strength, with all our soul, all our mind, and all our heart![9]

PER CRUCEM AD LUCEM (THROUGH THE CROSS TO THE LIGHT)

It's not a surprise that Padre Pio's spiritual direction focuses on the cross. We know that the three loves of Padre Pio were the cross, the Eucharist, and the Blessed Mother. The mysticism of the cross is central in Padre Pio's spirituality, and he learned this truth not from books and theology, but from his daily life's experience as being co-crucified without a cross. He became, in his words: "The Cyrenean who carries the cross for everybody."[10]

Padre Pio in his letters not only speaks of the cross constantly, but he uses a typical phraseology of the cross, for instance:

- The cross
- Calvary
- Sufferings of the body and soul
- Trials of every kind
- Aridity
- Anguish
- Shadows
- Temptation
- Tribulation
- Doubts and uncertainties
- The victim
- The interior martyrdom
- Fears
- Persecutions

This list is not simply a random choice of words, but each word or expression has a very powerful meaning in specific occasions and circumstances. He also uses allegoric words and expressions, like "Jewels," "Jewels of the Bridegroom," "Trials of the soul," "Necklaces of the only Begotten become man." The cross in any shape or form becomes the condition *sine qua non* of any spiritual journey. "Whoever has chosen the excellent part of divine service, must experience all the sufferings of Christ to a greater or lesser degree. And blessed are those souls who will be found more in conformity with the Divine Prototype, by having more greatly participated in His holy suffering!"[11]

The reason behind the *Per crucem ad lucem* is the cross,

which is a purifying suffering, the basis of spiritual direction in Padre Pio's methodology. "The prototype, the example on which one should reflect and model oneself, is Jesus Christ. But Jesus chose the cross as His standard, so He wants all His followers to tread the path to Calvary, carrying the cross and then dying stretched out on it. Only this way do we reach salvation."[12]

So, Padre Pio proposes the inner power of the Passion of Christ, connected with total renunciation to his spiritual daughters who, even though they experienced weaknesses of the body, also had the strength of the spirit and the theological virtues: "Jesus glorified is beautiful; but even though He is such in that state, He seems to me to be even more beautiful crucified."[13]

The development of Pio's methodology unfolds from passive resignation to active and dynamic cooperation in the work of redemption and salvation of humanity, through our personal and loyal behavior, almost reechoing the statement of Saint Paul: "Now I rejoice in my sufferings for your sake, and in my flesh I complete what is lacking in Christ's afflictions for the sake of his body, that is, the Church" (Col 1:24).

SALVA NOS, PERIMUS (SAVE US, WE ARE PERISHING)

This stage of spiritual direction is about intimacy; however, before getting to it, we must create an interior peace. That is not easy in our agitated, disorderly, violent, and arrogant society today, and it was not easy at the time of Padre Pio, when war, famine, and violence were rampant. In this turmoil, the friar seemed to have found the right prescription: "You know, my dear daughter, that the remedy which I willingly prescribe is tranquility of spirit, and that I always forbid excessive worry. You must endeavor to place your soul, agitated through the work of the evil spirit, in this state of rest and tranquility, reminding yourself of the spiritual rest which our hearts must always have in the will of

God, wherever it takes us."[14]

Padre Pio proposes three methods to handle *Salva nos, perimus.*

First, obedience to the spiritual director: Authority and guidance are very much needed in any stormy navigation. A spiritual director knows how to handle the waves and how to bring a ship safely into port. Padre Pio uses the evangelical event, when Christ seemed to sleep on the lake of Gennesaret, to illustrate the truth that the ship will not sink or go adrift if the captain (Jesus) is on board.

> Tell me once again, my dear daughters, what are you afraid of? Oh, don't you hear God saying to Abraham and to you: "Do not fear; I am your protector" [Gn 15:1]? What do you seek on earth, O daughters, if not God? You already possess Him. Therefore, be firm in your resolutions; stay in the ship in which He has placed you, and let the storm and hurricane come. Long live Jesus! You will not perish. He may sleep, but in the right place and at the right time He will wake up to restore the calm.
>
> Therefore, my daughters, do not fear, you are walking on the sea amidst the wind and waves, but with Jesus.
>
> What is there to fear then? But if fear takes you by surprise, exclaim strongly with St. Peter, "Oh Lord, save me!" [Mt 8:25; Mk 4:38; Lk 8:24]. He will stretch out His hand to you; hold on to it tightly and walk joyfully. Let the world turn upside down; let everything be in darkness, smoke, and noise. God is with us. But if God lives amidst the darkness and on a smoking Mount Sinai, covered with lightning, thunder, and noise, won't we be fine close to Him?[15]

Second, the teaching of the master: Padre Pio motivated his spiritual daughters with sound reasons based on moral theology and psychology. For instance, the feminine aspect of spirituality was at work when he explained with firmness and charity to the soul tightly gripped by doubts, uncertainties, or scruples, that we do not necessarily commit sin, when we try our best to follow the teacher, Jesus Christ.

> My daughter, do not fear the storm that roars about you, because in proportion to the rigidity of the winter, the spring will be more beautiful and richer in flowers and the fruits more abundant. No matter what the tempter may say or do, God is working out in you His admirable purpose, which is your sanctification. Do not believe the murmurings and promptings of the enemy, my beloved daughter, just stick firmly to the truth of what I am telling you with full authority as your director and all certainty of conscience. Do not believe Satan's suggestion that I just say this simply to comfort your soul. I do so certainly to comfort your soul, but this comfort is based on reality and truth.
>
> If I were to speak differently, I would wrong reality and would lie. Have I made myself clear? To be afraid of being lost while you are in the arms of divine goodness is stronger than fear on the part of a child in its mother's arms.
>
> Banish all doubt and anxiety which are, however, allowed by infinite love for the purpose already mentioned.[16]
>
> Be patient and do not become discouraged if you see yourself still full of imperfections. Remember what I said to you in this regard and make every effort to put it into practice.

When you are unable to take big steps on the path that leads to God, be content with little steps, patiently waiting until you have the legs to run; or, better still, wings to fly. Be content, my good daughter, with being, for now, a little bee in a hive which will soon become a big bee capable of producing honey. Lovingly humble yourself before God and man, because God speaks to the humble.[17]

Love silence because much talk is never without sin [see Prv 10:19]. Withdraw into yourself as much as you can, because in this way the Lord speaks freely to the soul, and the soul is more able to listen to His voice: Cut down on your visits to people and bear those visits made to you in a Christian manner.[18]

Third, the experience of the dark night: The role of the spiritual director guiding one through an experience of the dark night is one of utmost importance because the suffering can reach the atrocious point of martyrdom, and even bring the soul to the point of desperation. The spiritual director's role, then, is to convince the directee that what is taking place is the will of God — that God permits it — and therefore it should be embraced with love.

Go beyond this, I beg you, think of the great abandonment our Lord suffered in the Garden of Olives and observe this beloved Son asking the Father for some relief, but knowing the Father doesn't want to grant Him this, He thinks no more of it, nor does He ask this any longer; but as if He had never expected it, He bravely and courageously undertakes the work of our redemption. In moments of extreme distress, pray to the heavenly Father, that He may comfort and console you. If He is not pleased to do this, think of it no more, but arm yourself with new courage and undertake the work of your salvation on the cross, as if you were never to descend from it and were never to see your life becoming serene for you again. What do you expect, my daughter? We must speak to and see God amidst the thunder and the hurricane; we must see Him in the bush, amidst the fire and thorns. My daughter, to do this, it is necessary to go barefoot, and entirely renounce your will and affections.[19]

We may point out here that on November 8, 1916, Pio wrote to Padre Benedetto: "I am convinced that I must speak to You (God) in the midst of thunder and hurricanes, that I should see You in the burning bush amid the fire of tribulations, but to do all this I see that it is necessary to take off one's shoes and give up entirely one's own will and affections."[20]

Padre Pio, as a skilled spiritual director, goes even further into the dark night experience as a sign of God's love: "In the apostolic college there were those who loved and those who were loved. But all, except for the son of perdition, were loved by the divine Master. Not all were treated in the same manner, but according to their needs, characters, and capabilities. But all were chosen by the Redeemer. Therefore, be tranquil in God's holy name, and despise everything that upsets you, because it does not come from God."[21]

Having gone through the methodology used by Padre Pio in directing his spiritual daughters, we may ask an important question: "Can spiritual direction be done by correspondence?" Today we may include Facebook, Instagram, Twitter, email, texting, and so on. Any spiritual director will tell you that seeing and talking to the person one-on-one is the normal process of spiritual direction. However, in Pio's era, when these correspondences took place (1910–1923), a physically present engagement of prayer and counsel was not always possible due to war, confining illnesses, lack of public transportation, and the like. Therefore, spiritual guidance by correspondence became a sole and necessary option. It worked beautifully for Padre Pio, as we will see, in the insights and spiritual exchanges between the director and his spiritual daughters.

21

To Giovina Cerase

Pietrelcina, 14 October 1915

Dear Giovina,

May the grace of the Heavenly Father continue to assist you in the harsh trial through which you are passing through His goodness alone.

I am extremely happy for the divine grace of being able to see your longed-for and precious writing once again.

May God preserve us in His grace, and please me by allowing me to meet you personally when He wishes.

Infinite thanks for keeping me informed on all the concerns of our very dear Raffaelina, and I hope that you will continue to keep me informed of her state, until the poor thing is able to do so herself.

I am by no means surprised at the way she bore everything with indescribable serenity. It could not have been otherwise; her virtue, thank heaven, is quite well known to me. Only at the school of the Nazarene, my good Giovina, can one learn a lot in short time. This school, and no other, can make true heroines of the gentle sex. May God and His saints be blessed for revealing so many things to us!

You too, take heart, as all will work out for the glory of God and the salvation of souls. I will not fail in my duty to beseech, *usque ad noiam* ["to the point of annoyance"], the divine Heart, that he may soon bring an end to so much martyrdom.

You, too, remember me always in the treasure of your prayers, and know that your spiritual rather than your bodily health is and must be dear to my heart.

I will not forget you both in my poor prayers, nor all those who pray for me as you do.

With all the faith I have in my heart, I wish you every heavenly happiness.

Believe that I am always,

Your servant,

Fra Pio, Capuchin

22

To Annita Rodote

San Giovanni Rotondo, 31 December 1920
J.M.J.D.F.C.[1]

My dearest daughter,

My return wish for you is that the light of the divine mystery of God become Man may fill your heart and never abandon you, if that is best for your soul!

Your bad days would not be such even if night were to fall because "Even the darkness is not dark to you, for darkness is as light with you. The night is bright as the day" [Ps 139:12], just as it happened in Bethlehem.

Why then do you worry? I laugh at your suffering as you, many times, laughed at mine. Thus, each one laughs and cries, confirming, in this case also, what the book of Proverbs says: "Even in laughter the heart is sad" [Prv 14:13]. If you can, laugh at yourself with me and pray that I too can laugh at myself with you.

Cast aside worries, dismiss harmful judgments. God is in you and with you. What, then do you fear? The anguished fear of having lost him is a sure and evident sign that he dwells within you. Your soul seeks and does not find, so it suffers, flounders, becomes delirious and exhausted, without ever calming itself down in its despondency. But if, for one single minute, it could observe the satisfaction with which he observes your dissatisfied love, what joy! Nevertheless, you still feel that ardent desire to have Him always by your side, veiled and hidden! Yes, because a strong and generous heart, seeing how Love enjoys anxieties, would desire nothing but that enjoyment, and would happily be consumed in the briars of perpetual desolation.

Give my regards to all the sisters and I recommend myself to all their prayers. You must not dispense yourself from praying to Jesus for me, being aware of my many needs. Poor me! If God does not always help me, I will be crushed under the weight of my responsibilities, and those of other souls.

I bless you with redoubled paternal affection.

Most affectionately in the Lord,

Padre Pio of Pietrelcina[2]

23
To Margherita Tresca

San Giovanni Rotondo, 12 May 1921
J.M.J.D.F.C.

My always dearest daughter,

May Jesus always be totally yours and may He render you more and more worthy of His divine embraces!

I warmly thank you for the greetings on my name-day, and I thank you even more for the prayers you said for me. In return, I implore copious blessings for you from divine mercy. Always be better and do your best not to displease Jesus in anything.

Do not doubt my assistance, and don't attribute my inability to write to you, more often and at greater length, to carelessness. I have no time. My energy is constantly taken up with the needs of my brothers and sisters in exile.

Meanwhile, stay firm in your vocation, and do not worry about the future. Be calm and recommend my poor soul to Jesus, and the souls of all those who belong to me.

I bless you with paternal and redoubled affection.
Sincerely in Jesus,
Padre Pio of Pietrelcina

24
To Maria Gargani

San Giovanni Rotondo, 22 November 1916
J.M.J.D.F.C.

Most beloved daughter of Jesus,
May the grace of the Holy Spirit always guide your heart and transform it completely!

I received your letter and in it, my dear daughter, I perceived a good reason to bless Jesus for your soul, in which He has placed a great indifference in effect, if not in sentiment. These are a few words of consolation for you.[1]...

Courage, therefore, my dearest daughter. Live entirely in Our Lord and be tranquil. When you happen to violate the laws of indifference where indifferent matters are concerned, due to an impulse of self-love and our passions, as soon as you can, prostrate your heart before Jesus and humbly say to Him: "Lord have mercy, as I am weak." Then get up peacefully and calm yourself, and with holy indifference, carry on with your tasks.

We must behave in those times of struggle as a violinist usually behaves. Whenever the poor person notices a discordance, he neither breaks the string nor gives up playing the violin, but he immediately lends his ear to discover from where the discordance comes. Then he patiently tightens or loosens the string accordingly.

Well then, you too behave in this way. Do not become impatient at such wearisome matters, nor should you desire to break the string whenever you notice some discordance. But patiently humble yourself before God. Gently tighten or loosen the string of your heart before the heavenly Musician, in order that He might reorganize the concert.

I end, my beloved daughter, by thanking you on behalf of Jesus, for the prayers you say to Him for me. Multiply those prayers for me especially in this my hour of trial. I feel completely disconcerted at these trials which I will have to face shortly. Woe to you if you do not obtain from God and the divine Mother, the grace you know of. You, also, do me the charity of beginning the novenas to the Virgin of Pompeii, along with the entire recitation of the holy Rosary, receiving daily Communion for this reason also.

Tomorrow, please God, I will celebrate a Mass for you in thanksgiving to the divine Majesty for the favors lavished on your soul, and for your progress in the ways of the Lord.

I must present myself once again on the 8th of next month and, on that day, you too renew the offering to God, of which you spoke to me.

When you need to write to me, send your letter to Pietrelcina, Province of Benevento, and my family will see that I get it.

Goodbye, my good daughter, I cordially bless you.
Fra Pio

25
To Assunta Di Tomaso

San Giovanni Rotondo, 26 May 1917
J.M.J.D.F.C.

Dearest Assunta,

May the grace of the divine Spirit superabound in your heart and render you always more worthy of the glory of the blessed!

I beg you, my dearest daughter, not to think that due to forgetfulness or lack of affection I delayed so much in writing to you. In truth, the good will to serve God faithfully which I saw in your soul, aroused in me the greatest desire to help you with all my strength, apart from my duty which assists me and the inclination I have always had for your spiritual perfection, due to the regard I have had for you since I first met you.

Come on, my beloved little daughter, you must cultivate this well-formed heart carefully and spare nothing which could be useful to its happiness. Even though in every season — that is at every age — you can and must do this, your present age is the most suitable.[1]

Oh, my good daughter, it is a great grace to be able to serve this good God when youth renders one susceptible to everything! Oh, how this offering by which one offers the first fruits of the tree, is appreciated. And what can restrain you from making a total offering of your entire self to the good God, by deciding, once and for all, to give the world, the devil and the flesh a kick, as our godparents did for us in a determined manner when they held us at Baptism? Perhaps the Lord does not deserve this further sacrifice from you? We will discuss this again at a better time.

Meanwhile, live joyfully in God and for God. Believe that I love you very much before Jesus and I remain always

Your humble servant,

Fra Pio, Capuchin

While reading Padre Pio's letters to his spiritual daughters, we may treasure the variety and abundance of themes, developed as the spiritual direction goes on. The editors of the letters, Melchiorre of Pobladura and Alessandro of Ripabottoni, have some good insights about Padre Pio's letters.

By this, we do not mean to affirm that his letters — even the more involved and doctrinal ones — are original, critical, and wide statements, which he sometimes called "poor instructions" (724) or "lessons" (729). But one cannot deny that they are synthetic enunciations and truths; rapid writings from a pen dipped in scripture, theology, experience, and good sense. His preparation became more intense and diligent in accordance with the importance and complicated nature of the problems to be dealt with, and the more complex the sociological and spiritual state of the moment through which the souls were passing; even though the time available but rarely permitted him to write at length, as he would have wished. Suffice it to read, for example, his thoughts on the authentic love of God (675, 725); on true piety and authentic Christian perfection (687); on aridity, desolation of the spirit and spiritual trials (176–182, 668–669) and some maxims "to constantly live a devout life" (829–834).

Without theorizing or philosophizing on the subjects proposed in the exposition, there stands out a clear and precise knowledge of both ascetic and mystical spiritual phenomenology of the complicated plots of devout and pious practices, active and passive purgation, infused and acquired contemplation, locutions and visions, illusions, hallucinations. ... The diagnosis he makes in these cases and others of this nature, show knowledge of the phenomena described, and also reveal his personal experience.[2]

26

To Lucia Fiorentino

The relationship of Lucia Fiorentino with Padre Pio seems to be part of the Spiritual Diary which she wrote in 1929. Here is a description of a vision:

> In the vision I saw a tree of immeasurable size in the vestibule of our Capuchin Friary, and I heard a voice say to me: "This is the symbol of a soul which is now far away but will come here. He will do a great deal of good in this village. ... He will be strong and will have strong roots like this tree, and all those souls who come — both from here and from far away — if they take refuge in the shade of this tree, will be freed from evil: that is, whoever comes to this worthy priest for enlightenment, to find forgiveness and to make amends for their sins. If they humble themselves, they will receive advice and fruits of eternal life from this worthy priest. Woe to those who despise his advice, his behavior; the Lord will severely punish them in this life and the next. His mission will extend throughout the whole world, and many will come to take refuge in the shadow of this mystical tree, to receive the fruits of grace and forgiveness."[1]

• • •

San Giovanni Rotondo, 12 August 1917
J.M.J.D.F.C.

Dear Lucietta,

May your heart and those of all souls belonging to
Jesus always be possessed and permeated by divine love.
May this wish of mine always be realized in you, who are
so eager to love our most sweet heavenly Father.

As regards what you told me in your letter, I wish to
state, that even though I respect the judgment of your
confessor,[2] I do not share his opinion at all. He wants to
attribute the phenomenon you are experiencing in these
days to a purely natural cause, whereas I declare in the
Lord that it is a completely supernatural and divine phenomenon. Therefore, be tranquil and fear nothing. Let
the Lord work freely in you. Suffer patiently and offer
your suffering to the Lord.

You need do nothing to your body. Offer your spiritual suffering to Jesus, as it is more pleasing to Him.
Remember that this is the martyrdom also experienced
by the saints. You also, exclaim in that state with Saint
Teresa: "I die because I don't die."[3]

Meanwhile, live totally in God and, for the love He
has for you, bear yourself in all your miseries. Humble
yourself a great deal, my dear daughter, and confess that
if God were not your armor and shield, you would immediately be pierced with all kinds of sin. Therefore,
you must always keep yourself in the grace of God by
persevering in devout practices. Every day I present
your heart to the divine Father, along with that of His
most holy Son, during holy Mass. Given this union, by
virtue of which I make the offering, He could not reject
it. I am sure that you do the same. My dearest daughter,

I desire the peak of holy perfection for you in the heart of Jesus, and in Him, I bless you and cordially take my leave of you.

Your humble servant,
Fra Pio, Capuchin

27

To Rachelina Russo

[No date or address]
J.M.J.D.F.C.

My dearest Rachelina,

May Jesus totally possess your heart and render you worthy of his singular predilection!

My dearest daughter, what do you want me to say to you about the return of your miseries, if not that when the enemy returns, we must once again take up both our arms and courage to fight more than ever. I don't see anything of great importance in your letter. But dear God! above all else, beware of becoming somewhat diffident, because heavenly goodness permits similar weaknesses not to abandon you, but to render you humble and more steadfast, firmer and more tightly attached to the hand of His divine mercy. You will please God in a supreme manner, and me also, by not failing to carry out your devout practices in times of interior aridity and languor which often return to you. Because if you don't want to serve and love God simply for love of Him, and as the service we render Him amidst the sufferings of aridity is more pleasing to Him than that which we render Him amidst sweetness, we must likewise receive them willingly, at least with our superior will; and even though in accordance with our tastes and self-love this sweetness and tenderness appears to be more sweet to us, in accordance with God's tastes, aridity is more useful just as dry food is better for people with dropsy than liquid, even though they enjoy the latter more ... I bless you with paternal affection and my spirit is always in your midst.

Padre Pio

28

To the Ventrella Sisters

Here is a description of how the Ventrella sisters met Padre Pio for the first time:

> We understood we were before a religious of exceptional virtue: the goodness that transpired from his face and his limpid countenance immediately made an impression on our hearts. We were attracted to him by an indescribable force, and almost every day we went to him to recommend ourselves to his prayers and to ask his advice. In the beginning we addressed him in the polite form "lei" (thou), but he immediately said: "But what is this? You may use "tu" (you).

• • •

Naples, First Medical Clinic, 8 March 1918
J.M.J.D.F.C.

Dearest Vittorina,

May Jesus comfort, give sustenance and compensation in time and for blessed eternity, not only for me, but also for you and all those souls whom I love with paternal tenderness.

I have addressed this poor writing of mine to you; however, it is not only for you, but it is also for Maddalena and your sisters who are equally dear to me in the Lord.

I am aware of all your difficulties and infirmities, those of these days also, and do not think I remain behind the scenes as if I had nothing to do with your battles and cries. I tell you (and let nobody consider me to be stupid in this), as I have all the reasons to be such, that if you truly wish to believe I am a fool, do so, because it does not matter, as long as you listen to what I feel I must say to you.

Who is weak and I am not weak? [2 Cor 11:29] That is, who amongst you was weak in faith and virtue, that I did not go down to her level to encourage and help her, becoming everything to everyone, moaning and suffering with her? Who is scandalized that I do not burn? That is, was there anyone amongst you who, having fallen into some harm due to her weakness, did not see my holy anger against those who had absolutely no regard for the conscience of this poor soul, dragging into evil, and that I do not still burn with such a most bitter suffering for the harm caused to the person who fell?

But enough of this, because if it is necessary to feel proud, I will boast of those matters that concern my weakness. Do not believe, my daughters, that by being unable to express yourselves to your guide, that he is unaware of what takes place in your souls. If that were the case, you would be making a big mistake. Well, for the love of heaven, try as best you can to adhere to what I told you "Viva voce" ("what I told you in person") and in writing, because I said everything to you in the Lord.

You all know and understand well that lethargy, languor and shriveling of the senses cannot take place without its being followed by sensual sadness. But if your will and hearts are determined to belong totally to God, there is nothing to fear because they are natural imperfections, or rather, illnesses, and are not at all what you falsely want to believe: sins and spiritual failings.

Despite this, you must have great courage along with great activity of the spirit, as far as you possibly can.

Oh, how burdensome this mortal life is to the children of God! But the next life, which the mercy of the Lord will be pleased to grant us, dear God, will be more than we could desire. We certainly must not doubt our possessing it one day, even though we are so sinful; and if we are not so sinful it is simply because God is merciful towards those who place all their hope in him. When the holy Cardinal Borromeo was about to end his career, he had the crucifix brought to him to make his departure sweeter, with the sight of the Lord.

Therefore, when you find yourselves exposed to some trial or other, either physical or moral, bodily or spiritual, the best remedy is to think of Him who is our life, and never to think of the one without the other. Dear God, my dearest daughters, I beg you not to examine whether what you did, what you do and what you will do, was, is and will be very little, if it was done well or badly. Merely abstain from sin and from those actions which you clearly see to be sinful and do all with an upright conscience and with the will to please God [see 2 Cor 13:7].

My daughters, try as best you can, without excessive anxiety, to do what you must and wish to do with perfection. But once it is done, think no more about it, but rather, attend only to what you must and want to do or to what you are doing. Walk with simplicity in the ways of the Lord and do not torment your spirit. You must hate your faults, but with a quiet hate, not troublesome and restless. We must be patient with them and gain from them through holy humility.

Without that patience, my good daughters, instead of diminishing, your imperfections will increase constantly, as there is nothing that nourishes our defects like restlessness, and the haste to drive them away. Remember, my daughters, that I am the enemy of useless desires no less than I am of dangerous and bad desires. Because even though one's desires are good, nevertheless the desire is always defective in our regard, especially when it is combined with excessive haste, because God does not expect this sort of good, but He wants to practice another.

He wants to speak to us in the midst of the thorns, the bush, the cloud, and the lightning, like He did to Moses [see Ex 3:2; 19:16], and we want Him to speak to us in a sweet and fresh aura, as he did to Elijah [1 Kgs 19:12–13].

I end here, because I have had a fever for two days now, and it shows no sign of abating. May the will of God be done always! I have been here in the First Medical Clinic since yesterday, deprived of the one and only comfort that remains in me, that is, I am unable to offer the holy sacrifice of the Mass.[1]

Up to now everything has gone well and let us hope it continues in this way right to the end. Meanwhile, increase your prayers, beg the hearts of the Son and Mother, because you might as well know that Satan is trying to confuse matters.

Regards to your father and your aunt. Kiss Pierino for me and greetings to all the souls.

I warmly bless you and take my leave of you.

The most affectionate servant of your soul,

Padre Pio, Capuchin

29

To Erminia Gargani

San Giovanni Rotondo, 15 February 1918
J.M.J.D.F.C.

My dearest daughter,

May Jesus always be at the center of your heart and render you always more worthy of his favors.

I repeat that your soul's disposition is excellent. It aspires to a high degree of perfection which you can reach, and makes one understand the special love God has for you.

Thank Him for this with profound recognition, as we could desire no more precious gift from Him.

Therefore, my daughter, always resolve to generously correspond to grace, rendering yourself worthy of Him, that is, similar to Him in his adorable perfections, so well-known from the Scripture and the Gospel.

But to achieve this, we must reflect every day on His life. From reflection and meditating is born an esteem for His actions, and from esteem springs the desire to imitate Him along with the consolation gained from this.[1]

You must principally insist based on Christian justice and the foundation of goodness; that is, on the virtues which one deliberately tries to imitate, i.e., humility [see Mt 11:29], interior and exterior; more felt than shown, more profound than visible. My beloved daughter, consider yourself to be what you truly are: nothing, miserable and weak, source of boundless perversity, capable of converting good into evil, of attributing good to yourself, of justifying yourself in evil and, for love of the same evil, despising the Supreme Good.

With this conviction imprinted in your mind, my daughter:

1. You will never be pleased with yourself.
2. You will never complain of offenses wherever they come from.
3. You will excuse everyone in Christian charity.
4. You will always groan as a poor one before God.
5. You will not be surprised at all at your weakness, but recognizing yourself for what you are, you will blush at your inconstancy and infidelity to God, and you will trust in Him, abandoning yourself tranquilly in the arms of the Heavenly Father, like a child in the arms of its own mother.
6. Never ever, be exalted at your virtues, but repeat that everything comes from God, and to him give the honor and the glory.

This is enough for this lesson.

I approve of the proposition of immolating yourself to God with the vow of chastity, but it would be prudent to make it on a temporary and not perpetual basis. I think for 6 months, or at most, a year. You could use this formula: "I make a vow and promise Almighty God, the most holy Virgin Mary, my Guardian Angel, and the Seraphic Father Saint Francis, to observe the vow of chastity for the period of …"

I feel unwell physically and morally, and as the time for my presentation to the military draws closer, I feel the agony in my soul increasing. ...

And to render the heart of God more favorable, I would like you to make the vow of chastity on March 6, the day I must present myself. [2]

30

To Antonietta Vona

On the triduum of Antonietta's death in San Giovanni Rotondo on November 19, 1949, Padre Pio dictated the following thought as a remembrance: "She was one of those few souls with whom God was pleased. She lived in a hidden manner, in the most profound humility and in a state of continual suffering which she bore with a serene and joyful soul, and she died like a little candle, totally consumed in God and for God in whom she now rests for eternity."[1]

San Giovanni Rotondo, 20 March 1918
J.M.J.D.F.C.

May Jesus continue to possess your heart!

I read your letter and from its entirety I noticed that your state of soul is one of desolation or holy spiritual suffering.

To be more specific, I assure you:

a) That the recognition of your interior unworthiness is an extremely pure divine light with which your very being, and the potentiality to commit any crime whatsoever, without divine grace, is given to you to consider. That light is a result of the great mercy of God and was granted to the most excellent saints because it shelters the soul from all feelings of vanity and pride, and consolidates humility, which is the foundation of true virtue and Christian perfection; Saint Teresa also received this knowledge and said that it is so painful and horrible that it would cause death if the Lord did not sustain the heart.

b) The knowledge of one's potential unworthiness must not be confused with that of true unworthiness. The former renders the creature pleasing in the eyes of the Most High, and the latter renders it detestable, because it is the reflection of the iniquity present in the conscience. In the shadows in which you are present, you mistake the one for the other, and by knowing what you could be, you fear you are already that which is only possible in you.

c) Your being unaware of whether you are worthy of love or hate is suffering and not a chastisement, because nobody fears being unworthy when he truly wants to be such. That uncertainty is permitted by God to all the living, in order that they might not presume too much and thus they advance cautiously. It is especially permitted to you that you might find the cross and all its consequential merits in this torment. If you were always certain of divine love, what would you suffer? What suffering and what merit would your soul be given with a similar persuasion? Even the cruelest martyrdom would become a joy.

d) Even that resignation and aversion you believe you feel in this state of desolation is suffering. The spirit submits itself, but the lower nature becomes agitated, and it appears to you that even the spirit has rebelled.

e) God can reject everything in a creature conceived in sin, which carries the indelible mark inherited from Adam, but He absolutely cannot reject the sincere desire to love Him. So, if you cannot be sure of His heavenly mercy for any other reason, you must at least convince yourself of this.

In conclusion, you can and must be tranquil and joyful, in your concern for me. For everything and everyone, I hold eternal gratitude before God.

At present I feel a little better physically, but I beg you not to worry about this because this is the surest path that leads me to Heaven, and you cannot struggle against this for me.

Give my regards to everyone at home, and I wish you and everyone a very happy Easter.

I bless you and wish you greater blessings.

Most affectionately in Christ Jesus,

Padre Pio, Capuchin

31
To Lauretta Albanese

San Giovanni Rotondo, 7 December 1917
J.M.J.D.F.C.

Dearest Lauretta,

I praise and bless the Lord for the consolation he gave you after such a long agony.

Oh, how good God is, my dearest Lauretta! It is true that He is good to all, but He is particularly good to those who place all their trust in Him.

Tribulation is more precious than gold and rest, to those whom God has chosen. "I would rather be door-keeper in the house of my God than dwell in the tents of wickedness" [Ps 84:10]. How during these days, you, too, have been in a state of extreme discouragement in the house of our Lord, because the agony that tortured your heart did not cause you to lose hope in divine goodness. On the contrary, you always conformed your will to that of God, and with your will, you assiduously dwelt on the holy mount of Calvary. So, the Lord wishes to reward the sadness you bore for love of Him.

I received your other letter and only now am I able to tell you why I did not reply. The Lord prevented me from doing so, as He wanted you also, like Abraham, who sacrificed His own son in His heart to avoid dis-obeying God's command [see Gn 22:1–19], He wanted you too. I mean, to receive news of the salvation of your son, when you had nothing left to sacrifice but him, just

as the angel of God saved Abraham's. ... I take my leave
of you and warmly bless you.

Padre Pio

32

To an Unidentified Person

The editors of Padre Pio's letters tell us that six letters of Padre Pio were written to unknown recipients.

> Despite our efforts, up to now we have been unable to sort them out anagraphically, and their context and contents gave us no better result.
>
> We have already said that some of Padre Pio's letters were kept in a disorganized manner, outside their envelopes, without precise indications as to the addresses. Whereas, on other occasions, letters of different people, without the recipients' names, were placed in the envelopes by mistake.
>
> We believe that most of the letters are addressed to the Villani sisters (Giuseppina and Emanuelina), fervent Tertiaries[1] from the little town of San Marco La Catola, who had an excellent spiritual relationship with Padre Pio's venerable directors, Padre Benedetto and Padre Agostino."[2]

• • •

Naples, 5 November 1917
J.M.J.D.F.C.

My dearest daughter in Jesus,
     May the grace of Jesus always prevail in your heart, and may it transform you totally with His holy love!

I received your letter in which I was extremely pleased to hear from you that Jesus continues to keep you on the cross beside him. I experienced great consolation in this, and if I perceive some beautiful changes in your soul, it is precisely due to the cross on which Jesus has kept you up to now. Therefore, my daughter, do not desire to descend from this cross because this would be the descent of the soul to the plains, where Satan lays traps for us. Oh, my dearest daughter, this life is short, and the reward for what one suffers is eternal.

Let us do good; let us adhere to the will of God. Let this be the star on which we rest our gaze throughout this navigation, because in that way, we cannot but reach the right port.

Thank you for your prayers to the Lord for my liberation, which has finally come about, as I have been granted four months leave and I will begin this leave as soon as I am able to travel.[3]

Write to me in San Giovanni Rotondo, where I will make my way.[4] Thank you for the stamps.

Give my regards to your sister and to Miss [Maria] Gargani and warmly blessing you, I remain

Your servant,

Padre Pio, Capuchin

33
To Rachelina Campanile

Rachelina Campanile, a native of San Giovanni Rotondo, was born on June 2, 1902. She obtained her teaching diploma and taught in the town's elementary schools. At the advice of Padre Pio, Rachelina (known as Nina) took a vow of virginity which she renewed annually on the feast of the Immaculate Conception. She died at the age of 95 on January 9, 1989.

San Giovanni Rotondo, 23 March 1919
J.M.J.D.F.C.

Dear Rachelina,

May Jesus always be with you; may he bless you and make you grow holy and studious!

I received your note and I thank you for the much-appreciated remembrance you have for me before the Lord. In return I will do nothing but always remember you in my humble, fervent, assiduous prayers before Jesus, that he may bless your studies. Try with divine [help] to study always and be certain that the good God will crown your work when the time is ripe.

Be docile to grace also. Often think what a great favor it is for a soul to be in the heart of religion, amidst the pleasure and caresses of God, and do not render yourself unworthy of this.

When you see your cousin, Pasqualino, do not fail to greet him warmly.

I warmly bless you and I am waiting to hear you

are always that which a young girl who wants to imitate and portray Jesus Christ (within himself), and who is destined to become a teacher of infantile souls, should be.

Most affectionately in the Lord,
Padre Pio, Capuchin

34

To Lucietta Campanile

Lucia (diminutive is *Lucietta*), became a widow at a young age, then thought of becoming a nun, but remained at home. Padre Pio wrote five letters to her, guiding her in her difficult spiritual journey.

San Giovanni Rotondo [no date]
J.M.J.D.F.C.

May Jesus continue to grant you His love, and may He increase it in your heart, transforming it totally in Him!

Why are you agitated and sad? Do not fear, Jesus is yours; Isn't this sufficient for you? Doesn't He want that you are suffering? Isn't it He who places your soul in an almost powerless state, for no other reason except that of letting your soul experience its nothingness, and therefore, penetrate it with an intimate feeling of humility?

Courage, therefore, my daughter, take heart. Do what you must do, paying no attention if you are unable to do it as you would like. Jesus sees the interior disposition and He rewards this.

I bless you paternally along with your sister.

Padre Pio

35

To Maria Campanile

Due to her more frequent familiarity with Padre Pio, in the Campanile family, Anna Maria (Mariannina, commonly called Nina) stands out because he wrote to her twenty-four letters. Padre Pio simply called her Maria. "This is your name!" he said to her on one occasion, and this was how he addressed her in his letters.

San Giovanni Rotondo, 31 May 1918
J.M.J.D.F.C.

My dearest daughter,

May the divine Spirit always fill and comfort your heart and those of all souls who love Him!

I did not reply earlier to your last letter due to lack of time, and you, "bad girl," did not understand this. If you clearly understood the sentiments with which my soul is filled for yours, you would undoubtedly spare similar tortures. May the Lord be merciful towards you, as I have always been.

What can I say in answer to that last letter of yours? I will leave the "redde rationem" ["to give a reason"] of Satan's victory over you for better times. So, I beg you to be tranquil.[1] Save your tears for another occasion. And now to us:

My good daughter, certain suffering cannot be consoled by natural means, and your present suffering is naturally inconsolable.

So? So, it is necessary to elevate oneself on high, in

order to reach the beginning and original cause of your suffering. Now the cause and origin of your suffering is Jesus, whom you have chosen as your portion: it is the salvation of souls, which caused you to implicitly immolate yourself to the justice of God. My dearest daughter, you must convince yourself that this is the case, because God alone can bestow this humanly inexplicable suffering on souls, while at the same time sustain the same afflicted souls who are nailed to the cross of His Son.

My daughter, there is nothing left for you to do except resign yourself to the divine will who wants it so and bless the hand that shakes your spirit and body, convinced that it is always the hand of Him who, even though He exercises His grace, at the same time does not forget He is our Father!

The most afflicted souls are those chosen by the divine Heart; rest assured that Jesus has chosen your soul to be the chosen one of His adorable Heart.

You must hide yourself in His Heart; you must pour out your desires in this Heart; you must live in this Heart the remaining days that providence will grant you; you must die in this Heart when the Lord wishes. I have placed you in this Heart; therefore, you live, are, and move in this Heart.

This in brief is the explanation of your soul's martyrdom.

Now you will understand, my good daughter, why the soul who has chosen divine love, cannot remain selfish in the Heart of Jesus, but feels itself burn also with love for its brothers and sisters, which often causes the soul to suffer agonies.

But how can all this take place? My daughter, it is not difficult to understand this, because given that the soul no longer lives its own life, but lives in Jesus who lives within the soul, it must feel, want and live of the same sentiments and wishes of Him who lives within it. And you know, my most beloved daughter, even if you learned of this at a late stage, of the sentiments and desires which animate the Heart of this divine Master, for God and humanity.

Let your soul suffer agonies for God and for your brothers and sisters who do not want to have anything to do with Him, because this is supremely pleasing to Him. Live tranquilly and let your bitterness be in peace [see Is 38:17].

My daughter, recommend me to divine mercy, I am about to be crushed under the weight of the trial. Alas, who will deliver me from this body of death [Rom 7:24]? I repeat, pray that I may become less wretched. Alas, my daughter, who can understand my interior martyrdom! The Lord is trying me in the waters of contradiction. Well! Help me with your prayers to the Lord. But is the Lord perhaps tired of me and for this reason has decreed my extermination![2]

How can you see a father suffer so much without being moved to pity?!

Both you and Girolama, whom I warmly bless, receive Holy Communion for me until further notice and say a novena to the Virgin of Pompeii for some graces I am awaiting.

I bless you and Girolama[3] in the name of the Seraphic Father, and once again assure you that your soul is pleasing to God.

Padre Pio

I beg you not to let your imagination run riot.

36
To Girolama Longo

San Giovanni Rotondo, 29 July 1920
J.M.J.D.F.C.

My dearest daughter,
May Jesus always be your Jesus and may He render you always more dear to Him!

The bitterness of love is still sweet and its weight suave. Therefore, why do you continually say, when feeling its great transports, that you are unable to contain it? Your heart is small, but it is expandable, and when it can no longer contain the grandeur of the Beloved, and resist its immense pressure, do not fear, because He is both inside and out; by pouring himself into the interior, He will surround the walls. Like an open shell in the ocean, you will drink your fill and, exuberantly, you will be surrounded and carried along by His power.

In a short while you will no longer be new to this new behavior of love, and its assaults will no longer be unbearable for you. Accustomed to the usual flames you will call it into competition, and you will struggle like Jacob with the angel [see Gn 32:22–32], without falling.

Do not complain if you are still unable to embrace the supreme Good. The time will come when you possess it totally.

Be tranquil as regards my health. I am well, thank God. I only recommend that you pray a great deal to Jesus for me that He might give me the strength to bear the weight which He is loading on me; enlightenment with which to guide souls and the grace to make me accomplish His divine will in a perfect manner.

All are well in your home. Carmela, Graziella[1] and your mother often came to the Friary, and they all approached the Sacraments. You can be pleased with this, isn't that so?

Give my regards to the Rev. Mother Superior and all the other sisters; I pray assiduously to Jesus for their spiritual progress. I expect the same charity from them.

Congratulations and felicitations from me to that very dear daughter, Sister Benedetta,[2] on her religious profession. Kindest regards to my sister.[3]

I warmly bless you.

Padre Pio

37

To Frieda Folger

The editors of the letters inform us that Frieda Folger was born in Wattwil (Switzerland) on May 30, 1868. She was a teacher and very much involved in Franciscan ministry when she became a Secular Franciscan. She started the Seraphic Mass Association and the Eucharistic Association for the Missions and for poor churches. She died on July 23, 1954. The official periodical of the Capuchin Order wrote about her life and ministry.[1]

San Giovanni Rotondo, 18 October 1922

Soul of the dear God,

May Jesus always be totally yours; may He always reign as King of your heart, assist you always in your good works and render you always more worthy of His divine embraces!

With these most sincere prayers which I say for you to Jesus, I reply to your last most welcome letter, to rejoice with you at the work that Jesus is carrying out through you. May Jesus always be blessed for this.

Meanwhile, do not let difficulties you encounter stop you from doing good. Jesus is with you, and you have nothing to fear. My spirit is always close to you. Therefore, do not fear.

Thank you for what you kindly sent me. May Jesus reward you greatly.

I bless you with paternal and redoubled affection, and I recommend myself to your prayers.

Padre Pio, Capuchin

38
To Elena Bandini

Besides the letters, there are more than a hundred little notes preserved, consisting of very short questions on the part of Elena to Padre Pio, and equally brief replies (almost telegraphic) from Padre Pio. Many notes are undated but were probably written after 1932 and were certainly delivered by hand. Elena was born in Borgo San Lorenzo (Florence), educated in Switzerland; she taught French and German; then she moved to San Giovanni Rotondo in 1937.

San Giovanni Rotondo, 25 January 1921

My dearest daughter,

May Jesus always be totally yours; may He look upon you always with benevolent eyes, assist you always in everything with His vigilant grace, guide you always in everything, and may He sustain you and make you holy!

With these most sincere prayers which I assiduously say for you to Jesus, I reply to your letter which you sent me through Miss Serritelli.[1] I am happy to hear you are always full of good will, and I render heartfelt thanks to God for this. Try more and more to make use of the talents you received from God.

Work assiduously for the salvation of our brothers and sisters and bring the spirit of Saint Francis to the knowledge of everybody; a spirit which is entirely that of Jesus Christ. Society needs to be reformed, and I know of no more efficacious means except that all should become Tertiaries of Saint Francis, and that they live with his spirit. On this condition and agreement, I number you amongst my dearest children.

Recommending myself and all those who belong to me, to your prayers, I bless you with paternal and redoubled affection.

Very sincerely in Jesus Christ,
Padre Pio of Pietrelcina

39
To Violante Masone

San Giovanni Rotondo, 19 May 1921
J.M.J.D.F.C.

Dearest Violante,

May Jesus always reign in your heart and over your family, and may He render you always more worthy of His divine love.

I received your letter and I render heartfelt thanks to God for the great desire He makes you feel to become better and better always. Therefore, I exhort you not to slow down or become lukewarm in that fervor which the Lord allows you to feel. Do not extinguish and do not suffocate the good inspirations that God sends you. Be a true apostle of good in that town, which is in great need of this. Do not abstain from doing good due to silly and useless apprehension. If there are foolish people who make fun of the work of the children of God, have a good laugh at them and continue to do the work you started. The divine Master has promised a reward not to those who begin well, but to those who persevere to the end [see Mt 10:22; 24:13]. Let the example of Judas be sufficient for you; he began well, continued to do good, but did not persevere to the end, so [he was] lost.

Tell Graziella[1] not to hesitate in joining the ranks of the Third Order. I believe the Lord wants to save our town through the institution of the Third Order of Saint Francis. So, beg the parish priest[2] and the treasurer to get to work, and Saint Francis will bless your families. Do not worry if there are only a few of you in the beginning. Make a start and you will see that the ranks will increase continually and God's blessing [will be copious]. Do not restrict the number of Tertiaries to young girls and women only, but embrace everyone, because that was Saint Francis' aim in this.

Regards to everyone and I recommend myself to everyone's prayers. I bless you with paternal and redoubled affection, and I remain,

Very sincerely in Jesus
Padre Pio

The editors of Padre Pio's letters, in volume 3, list fifty recipients of his letters during the period of 1915 to 1923. There are, however, more letters which the editors were not able to locate.[3]

For instance, one of these spiritual daughters was Giuseppina Morgera, who was born in Casamicciola (Island of Ischia) on January 1, 1885, and died in Genoa on July 27, 1974. On June 23, 1915, the noblewoman Raffaelina Cerase spoke to Padre Pio in a very flattering manner of this young woman.[4] Apart from anything else, Giuseppina was much esteemed in some Naples environments and so Raffaelina sought her influence to exonerate Padre Pio from military service, which he was undergoing in those days in Naples.[5] Giuseppina Morgera took this recommendation to heart, but, due to a lack of time, did not bring it to a conclusion.[6]

40
To Graziella Pannullo

San Giovanni Rotondo, 30 December 1921
J.M.J.D.F.C.

Dearest Graziella,

May Jesus always be totally yours; may He assist you always with His vigilant grace and make you totally in accordance with His divine Heart.

I received your most welcome letter, and I reply with some delay due to my many occupations during these days. What beautiful words I read at the beginning of your letter: "I am a daughter of Saint Francis along with fifty others." Good girl, you are right to be pleased, and you will be more and more pleased when your ardent zeal and profound piety, together with your illustrious example, will have attracted thousands to Saint Francis, so that Jesus will be glorified in him.

The Third Order of Saint Francis has always been, and is still, even more so today, an important factor in seeing that humanity returns to the light of faith, to the healthy principles of Christian morals. On the [seven] hundredth anniversary of the foundation of this Order,[1] this solemn remembrance was like a very great and most solemn recalling of all souls and also true spiritual enthusiasm for those who fight in a holy manner under the centuries-old banner of the Rule of Saint Francis.

Our town, which must be very dear to our hearts, will receive the choicest blessings from heaven, if it continues the beautiful work it has begun. However, a well-organized and assiduous propagation is necessary, enabling all to understand the great and noble goal, which is the sanctification of one's own soul, the reformation of society, the reformation of the family, spiritual graces and holy indulgences connected to this. Through your goodwill and the cooperation of others, you should, on some free day you have during the month, gather all your sisters and encourage them, with a little spiritual talk, to be faithful to the proposition made, by frequenting the Sacraments. You must assure them that, in the most holy Sacrament of the Eucharist, in the Sacrament of love, we have true life, a blessed life, and true happiness, because in it we receive, not only those graces that perfect us, but the very author of these graces. Our fathers[2] will not fail to give you their help. They will often come to break the bread of the Word of God with you, and in return, we will ask for nothing except your correspondence to God and Saint Francis, and docility towards the impulses of grace.

I hope that the day will not be far off when you will enjoy a taste of the joy of paradise, going to Assisi, which is a totally Franciscan town, a monument which speaks of the great love and infinite charity of our holy Father, Saint Francis. Yes, I hope that you will one day, in the not-too-distant future, be prostrated there, in the little devout temple of the Porziuncola, blackened with the wings of time, which throughout the seven centuries of religious admiration, the kisses of the penitents have worn away, as the good admirer of Franciscan works, Mrs. Henrion[3] narrates, so that the rough walls are almost marble and alabaster. Oh, how the heart of the pilgrim who pauses there to pray fervently beats at the remembrance! Every dark brick retells the story of thousands and thousands of souls who, in confident abandonment, rested their heads there in the anguish of life.

The pilgrim kneels there instinctively, and in divine silence feels some relief like a most sweet blessing, and infinite and sweet prayers resound and pass throughout the centuries, ardent with the love of the saints, holocaust of pure victims, tears of the redemption. Oh! how great, how sweet is the divine dogma of the Communion of Saints in the Church of Jesus! This truly is the door to eternal life, as it is written on the wall of the little devout temple of the Porziuncola.

Re-evoking the marvels of that period, the beloved first-born of the Seraphic Father comes to my mind; there in the deep and solemn silence of the austere refectory, Saint Clare, with her humble and mortified little daughters, who, to the rhythm of poverty, sing the short and clear notes of renunciation and sacrifice. Each one of the sisters takes her place, raises her mind to the Lord and waits in peace. ... Then the limpid voice of the Mother, Saint Clare, intones the "Benedicite" ["Bless me"]. The virginal hand slowly and solemnly raises itself in order to bless them with a great and miraculous gesture.

Once, there was nothing but a loaf of bread in the Monastery, and it was lunch time.[4] Their appetites burned the poor sisters' stomachs who, having triumphed over everything, still could not always ignore the imperious necessities of life. Sister Cecilia, the housekeeper, turned to the holy Abbess in this emergency, and she ordered the bread to be divided in two; to send half to their brothers, who were in the monastery and to keep the rest. This was then to be divided into fifty portions, in accordance with the numbers of sisters, and each sister was to be given her portion on the table of poverty. But, as the devout daughter replied that one of Jesus' miracles would be necessary for such a small amount of bread to be divided into fifty portions, the Mother Superior replied: "My daughter, do what I tell you with certainty."

The obedient daughter hastened to obey the maternal command, and Mother Clare immediately had recourse to Jesus through prayers and pitiful sighs for her little daughters. Through divine grace, the bread then increased in the hands of she who broke it, and each received a large portion.

Another day, the handmaid of the Lord had no oil, so that she could not even prepare the food for the ill sisters.[5] Then Saint Clare, a master of humility, took the container in her hand, washed it with her hands and placed it on the little wall, so that the friar alms-seeker could take it. Then she called him, in order that he might go in search of oil. Brother Bentivenga hastened to come to the needs of the poor sisters. But before he arrived, the container was filled with oil through divine mercy, as the prayers of Saint Clare, preceded the holy obedience of the holy Father (Brother Bentivenga) to relieve his poor daughters. And the friar, thinking that they had called him in vain, complained: perhaps the sisters called me to make fun of me, because the container was full. He sought somebody who could have brought the oil, but he found nobody. Thus, the Lord miraculously came to the aid of those who had abandoned everything for Him, and He bowed in an obedient manner to His bride's will who invoked Him with purity and with that faith that moved mountains.

Let us also ask our good Jesus for the humility, trust, and faith of our dear saint; let us pray fervently to Jesus like her. Let us abandon ourselves to Him, detaching ourselves from this lying world where everything is folly and vanity; everything passes, only God remains to the soul, if it knows how to love Him well. Those souls who throw themselves into the whirlpool of worldly preoccupations are poor and unfortunate. The more they love the world, the more their passions multiply, the more their desires are lit, the more they find themselves incapable of carrying out their projects, and thus they are uneasy, impatient, affected by that shock that breaks their hearts; those hearts which do not beat with charity and holy love. Let us pray for these unfortunate and miserable souls, that Jesus may forgive them and draw them to himself in His infinite mercy.

You who have received many gifts and graces from Jesus, continue to increase always in the life of virtue, and your piety and zeal will recall those who are far from the right path, and thus you will praise the Lord along with our common father, Saint Francis, in all the works of the creation, obtaining copious reward on earth and in heaven.

I beg you to give my regards to the parish priest [Don Salvatore Pannullo] and everybody else in the most sweet Lord. And in Him, believe that I am most affectionately,

Padre Pio, Capuchin

Happy new year. I ask for everybody's help through prayers.

Padre Pio in agony

Part 3
Non-Epistolary Writings

"Father, take this cup away from me ... not my will, but yours, be done."

(Luke 22:42)

41

Meditation on the Agony of Jesus in the Garden of Gethsemane

Most Divine Spirit, enlighten and inflame me in meditating on the Passion of Jesus, help me to penetrate the mystery of love and suffering of a God, Who, clothed with our humanity, suffers, agonizes and dies for the love of the creature. ... The Eternal, the immortal Who debases himself to undergo an immense martyrdom, the ignominious death of the Cross, amidst insults, contempt and abuse, to save the creature which offended Him, and which wallows in the slime of sin. Humans rejoice in their sin and God is sad because of sin, suffers, sweats blood, amidst terrible agony of spirit. No, I cannot enter this wide ocean of love and pain unless Thou with Thy grace sustain me. Oh, that I could penetrate to the innermost recesses of the Heart of Jesus to read there the essence of His bitterness, which brought Him to the point of death in the Garden; that I could comfort Him in the abandonment by His Father and His own. Oh, that I could unite myself with Him in order to expiate with Him.

Mary, Mother of Sorrows, may I unite myself with Thee to follow Jesus and share His pains and Thy sufferings.

My Guardian Angel, guard my faculties and keep them recollected on Jesus' suffering, so that they will not stray far from Him.

1

Arriving at the close of His earthly life, the Divine Redeemer, after having given himself entirely to us as food and drink in the Sacrament of His love and having nourished His Apostles with His Body and Blood, Soul and Divinity, went with His own to the Garden of Olives, known to His disciples and to Judas. Along the road which leads from the Cenacle to the Garden, Jesus teaches His disciples. He prepares them for the impending separation, for His imminent Passion, and prepares them to undergo, for love of Him, calumnies, persecution and death itself, to fashion in themselves Him, Who is their model.

"I shall be with you" and do not be troubled, O disciples, because the Divine promise will not fail. You will have a proof of this in the present solemn hour.

He is there to begin His dolorous Passion. Instead of thinking of himself, He is all anxiety for you.

Oh, what an immensity of love does this Heart contain! His face is covered with sadness and at the same time with love. His words proceed from His innermost Heart. He speaks with a profusion of affection, encouragement, comfort, and in comforting gives His promise. He explains the most profound mysteries of His Passion.

This journey of Thine, O Jesus, has always touched my heart with an increase of love so profound and so deep for those who love Thee, with increase of love that hurries to immolate itself for others, to ransom them from slavery. Thou hast taught there is no greater proof than to lay down one's life for one's friends. And now Thou art about to put this seal on the proof of Thine own life. Who would not be overawed by such an oblation?

Arriving at the garden, the Divine Master withdrew apart from His disciples taking along only three of them, Peter, James and John, to have them as witnesses of His sufferings. Just these three, who had seen Him transfigured on Tabor between Moses and Elias, and who had confessed Him to be God, would they now have the strength to acknowledge the Man-God in pain and mortal anguish?

Entering the Garden, He told them: "Remain here. Watch and pray that you enter not into temptation!" Be on your guard, He seems to say to them, because the enemy is not asleep. Arm yourself against him beforehand, with the weapon of prayer, so that you may not become involved and led into sin. It is the hour of darkness. Having thus admonished them, He separates himself from them about a stone's throw and prostrates himself on the ground.

He is extremely sad; His soul is a prey of indescribable bitterness. The night is advanced and bright. The moon shines in the sky, leaving shadows in the Garden. It seems to throw a sinister brightness, a foreboding of the grave and dreadful events to come, which make the blood tremble and freeze in the veins — it seems as if stained with blood. A wind, like the forerunner of the coming tempest, agitates the olive trees and, together with the rustling of the leaves, penetrates the bones, like a messenger of death, descending into the soul and filling it with deadly grief.

Night most horrible, like which there will never be another!

What a contrast, O Jesus! How beautiful was the night of Thy birth, when Angels, leaping for joy, announced peace, singing the Gloria! And now, it seems to me, they surround Thee sadly, keeping at respectful distance, as if respecting the supreme anguish of Thy spirit.

This is the place where Jesus came to pray. He deprived His most sacred humanity of the strength bestowed on it by His Divine Person, submitting it to indefinable sadness, extreme weakness, to dejection and abandonment, to mortal anguish. His spirit swims in these as a limitless ocean, and every moment seems about to be submerged. It brings before His spirit the entire sufferings of His imminent Passion, which, like a torrent that has overflowed its banks, pours into His Heart, torments, oppresses and submerges it in a sea of grief.

He sees first Judas, His disciple, loved so much by Him who sells Him for just a few coins, who is about to approach the Garden to betray Him and give Him over into the hands of His enemies. He! The friend, the disciple whom a little while before He had nourished with His Body and Blood ... prostrate before him, He had washed his feet and pressed them to His Heart. He had kissed those feet with brotherly affection, as if by sheer force of love, He wanted to hold him back from his impious, sacrilegious design, or at least, having committed the insane deed, he might enter himself, recalling so many proofs of love, and perhaps would repent and be saved. But no, he goes to his ruin and Jesus weeps over his voluntary perdition.

He sees himself bound and dragged by His enemies through the streets of Jerusalem, through those very streets through which only a few days before He passed triumphantly acclaimed as the Messiah. ... He sees himself before the High Priest beaten, declared guilty of death. He, the author of life also sees himself led from one tribunal to another, into the presence of judges who condemn Him.

He sees His own people, so loved by Him, the recipients of so many of His benefits, who now maltreat Him with infernal howls and hissing, and with a great shout, demand His death — the death on the cross. He hears their unjust accusations, sees himself condemned to the most awful scourging; crowned with thorns, derided, saluted as a mocking, and struck.

Finally, He sees himself condemned to the ignominious death of the cross, then ascending to Calvary, fainting under the weight of the cross, pale and falling to the ground repeatedly. He sees himself, arrived on Calvary, despoiled of His garments, stretched out on the cross, pitilessly crucified, raised up on it in the sight of all. He hangs on the nails which cause excruciating torture. ... Oh God, what a long agony of three hours will over-whelm Him amidst the insults of a crazed, heartless crowd.

He sees His throat and entrails on fire with a burning thirst, and to add to this agony, a drink of vinegar and gall. He sees the abandonment of His Father and the desolation of His Mother.

At the end, the ignominious death between two robbers; the one to acknowledge and confess Him as God and be saved, the other to blaspheme and insult Him and die in despair.

He sees Longinus approach and, as a final insult and con-tempt, pierce His side. Christ beholds the consummation of hu-miliation in the separation of soul and body.

Everything, everything, passes before Him, torments Him, terrifies Him, and this terror takes possession of Him, over-whelms Him. He trembles as if shaken by a violent fever. Fear also seizes Him, and His spirit languishes in mortal sadness.

He, the innocent Lamb, alone, thrown to the wolves, with-out any refuge. ... He, the Son of God ... the Lamb dedicated voluntarily to be sacrificed for the glory of the same Father Who abandoned Him to the fury of the enemies of God, for the re-demption of the human race; forsaken by those very disciples who shamefully flee from Him as from a most dangerous being. He, the Eternal Son of God, has become the laughingstock of His enemies.

But will He retreat? No, from the very beginning He em-braces everything without reservation. Why then and whence this terror? Ah! He has exposed His humanity as a target to take upon himself all the blows of divine justice offended by sin.

Vividly, He feels in His naked spirit all that He must suffer; every single pain, and He is crushed because He has given over His humanity as a prey to weakness, terror, fear.

He seems to be at the extremity of suffering. ... He is pros-trate with His face to the ground before the majesty of His Fa-ther. The Sacred Face of Him Who enjoys, through the hypostatic union, the beatific vision of the Divine Glory accorded to both Angels and Saints in Heaven, lies disfigured on the ground. My God! Jesus! Art Thou not the God of Heaven and earth, equal in all things to Thy Father, Who humiliates Thee to the point of losing even the semblance of man?

Ah, yes! I understand. It is to teach me, proud man, that to deal with Heaven, I must abase myself down to the center of the earth. It is to repair and expiate for my haughtiness, that You lie down before Thy Father. It is to direct His pitying glance upon humanity, which has turned away from Him by rebellion. It is because of Thy humiliation that He forgives the proud creature. It is in order to reconcile earth with heaven, that Thou abases Thyself down to it, as if to give it the kiss of peace. O Jesus, mayest Thou be blessed and thanked always and by all men for all Thy mortifications and humiliations by which Thou hast atoned for us to God to Whom Thou has united us in the embrace of holy love!

2

Jesus rises and turns His sad and suppliant glance to Heaven. He raises His arms and prays. My God, with what deadly pallor that face is suffused! He prays to that Father who seems to have turned away His glance and Who appears ready to strike Him with His sword of vengeance. He prays with all the confidence of a Son, but He fully understands the position He holds. He realizes that it is He alone, as a victim for the human race, who bears the odium of having outraged the Divine Majesty. He realizes that He alone, through the sacrifice of His life, can satisfy divine justice and reconcile the creature with the Creator. He wants it and wants it efficaciously. But nature is crushed at the sight of His bitter Passion. Nature revolts against the sacrifice. But His spirit is ready for the immolation, and He continues the battle with all His strength. He feels himself cast down, but He perseveres in the oblation of himself.

My Jesus, how can we obtain strength from Thee, if we see Thee so weak and crushed?

Yes, I understand. Thou hast taken all our weakness upon Thyself. And to give us Thy strength Thou hast become the scapegoat. It is to teach us that we must place our trust only in Thee in the struggles of life, even when it seems as if Heaven were closed to us.

Jesus in agony cries to His Father: "If it is possible, take this chalice from Me!" It is the cry of nature which, weighed down, confidently has recourse to Heaven for assistance. Although He knows that He will not be heard, because He wants it thus, He prays. My Jesus, why dost Thou ask that which Thou knows will not be granted? Suffering and Love.

Behold the great secret. The pain which oppresses Thee urges Thee to seek help and comfort, but the love to satisfy divine justice and give us back to God makes Thee cry out: "Not Mine, but Thy will be done!" To this prayer Divine Justice exacts the sacrifice necessary to repair the injury to God.

His desolate Heart has need of comfort. The desolation in which He finds himself, the battle which He is fighting alone, seems to make Him go in search of someone who could comfort Him. Slowly, therefore, He rises from the ground and, staggering takes a few steps. He approaches His disciples in search of comfort. They, having lived so long with Him, they, His confidants, could well understand His internal grief. And with this expectation He goes to them. They will surely know how to provide a little comfort for Him.

But oh, what a disillusionment! He finds them buried in profound sleep and feels himself so much more alone in that limitless solitude of His Spirit. He approaches them and, sweetly turning to Peter, He says: "Simon, dost Thou sleep? Thou who didst protest that thou didst want to follow Me unto death?"

and turning to the others He adds: "Could you not watch one hour with me?" The lament of the Lamb destined for sacrifice; of a wounded Heart that suffers immensely ... alone, without comfort. He, however, raises himself as if from a battlefield, and forgetting himself and His sufferings, concerned only for them, adds: "Watch and pray that you fall not into temptation." He seems to say: "If you have so quickly forgotten Me, who struggles and suffers, at least watch and pray for yourselves.

They, however, heavy with sleep, hardly hear the voice of Jesus; they barely perceive Him as a faint shadow, so much so that they are not aware of His countenance, all disfigured from the internal agony which tortures Him.

O Jesus, how many generous souls wounded by this complaint have kept Thee company in the Garden, sharing Thy bitterness and Thy mortal anguish. ... How many hearts in the course of the centuries have responded generously to Thy invitation. ... May this multitude of souls, then, in this supreme hour be a comfort to Thee, who, better than the disciples, share with Thee the distress of Thy heart, and cooperate with Thee for their own salvation and that of others. And grant that I also may be of their number; that I also may offer Thee some relief.

3

Jesus has returned to His place of prayer and another picture, more terrible than the first presents itself to Him. All our sins with their entire ugliness parade before Him in every detail. He sees all the meanness and the malice of creatures in committing them. He knows to what extent these sins offend and outrage the Majesty of God. He sees all the infamies, immodesties, blasphemies which proceed from the lips of creatures accompanied by the malice of their hearts, of those hearts and those lips which were created to bring forth hymns of praise and benediction to the Creator. He sees the sacrileges with which priests and faithful defile themselves, not caring about those Sacraments instituted for our salvation as necessary means for it; now, instead, made an occasion of sin and damnation of souls. He must clothe himself with this entire unclean mass of human corruption and present himself before the sanctity of His Father, to expiate everything with individual pains, to render Him all that glory of which they have robbed Him; to cleanse that human cesspool in which man wallows with contemptible indifference.

And all this does not make Him retreat. As a raging sea this mass inundates Him, enfolds Him, oppresses Him. Behold Him before His Father the God of Justice, facing the full penalty of divine justice. He, the essence of purity, sanctity by nature, in contact with sin! ... Indeed, as if He himself had become a sinner. Who can fathom the disgust that He feels in His innermost spirit? The horror He feels. The nausea, the contempt He senses so vividly? and having taken all upon himself, nothing excepted, He is crushed by this immense weight, oppressed, thrown down, prostrated. Exhausted, he groans beneath the weight of divine justice, before His Father, Who has permitted His Son to offer himself as a Victim for sin, as one accursed.

He would rather shake off this immense burden that crushes Him — He would fain free himself of this horrible load which makes Him shudder — His own purity rejects it — the very glance of the avenging Father, Who abandons Him in these muddy, putrid waters of guilt with which He sees himself covered — all this rushes to His Spirit urging Him to draw back from the bitter Passion. The revulsion of His Divinity against sin adds to the conflict within His human soul. All instinct counsels that He unburden himself of these infamies, rejecting the very thought of them. But the consideration of unvindicated justice and the unreconciled sinner predominates in His heart full of love. These two forces, these two loves, one holier than the other, struggle for victory in the Heart of the Savior. Which will conquer? Without doubt, He wants to give victory to the offended justice. This gains over all else and He wants this to triumph. But what a spectacle must He represent? That of a man soiled with the filth of humanity. He, essential sanctity, to see himself filthy with sin, even if only in outward appearance? This, no! This terrifies Him, makes Him tremble, crushes Him.

To find support in this terrible conflict He gives himself over to prayer. Prostrate before the majesty of His Father, He says: "Father, take this chalice from Me!" It is as if He said: My Father, I want Thy glory, I want Thy justice to be fully satisfied, I want the human family to be reconciled with Thee. But that I, Who am sanctity itself, should see Myself defiled by sin. Ah! Not this! Take away, therefore, take away this chalice, and Thou to Whom all is possible, find in the infinite treasures of Thy Holy Wisdom another means. But, if Thou dost not want this: Not my Will, but Thine be done!"

4

And again, this time the prayer of the Savior has no effect. He feels as if He were about to die. With difficulty, He raises himself from prayer in search of comfort. He feels His strength ebbing away. Tottering and grasping, He directs His steps towards His disciples. Again, He finds them sleeping. At this His sadness becomes deeper, and He is content merely to awaken them. What confusion must have overcome them! But Jesus says nothing this time. He only seems immensely sadder to me. ... He keeps to himself all the bitterness and pain of this abandonment and indifference. By His silence He seems to sympathize with the weakness of His own.

Jesus, how much pain I read in Thy Heart already full to overflowing with distress. I see Thee withdraw from Thy disciples, cut to the Heart. Ah, if I could give Thee some relief, some comfort. But, not knowing what else to do, I weep at Thy side.

The tears of my love for Thee and of my sorrow for my sins, conscious of Thy suffering, unite themselves to Thine. They can rise to the throne of the Father and incline Him to have pity on Thee and on so many souls who are sleeping the sleep of sin and death.

Again, Jesus returns to His place of prayer, afflicted, weakened. He falls rather than prostrates himself. A mortal anguish overwhelms Him and He prays more intensely. The Father turns away His glance as if He were the most abject of men.

I seem to hear all laments of the Savior: Oh, if at least man, for whom I am in anguish and for whom I am ready to embrace all, could only be "grateful," would respond to the graces I obtain for him by my great suffering for him! If he would only esteem the value of the price I pay to ransom him from the death of sin, to bestow on him the true life of the sons of God. Ah, that love which grieves my Heart more cruelly than the executioners will tear my flesh! … Oh no! He sees man who does not know because he does not want to draw profit from it. He will even blaspheme this Divine Blood, and more irreparable and inexcusable still, will turn it to his damnation. Only a few will profit by it; the great number run the way of perdition.

And in the great distress of His Heart, He continues to repeat: "*Quae utilitas in sanguine meo!*" "What profit is there in My Blood!" But even the thought of these few urges His Heart to continue to endure the conflict, to face all the sufferings of His Passion and death to obtain for them the palm of victory.

There remains nothing to which He can turn to find comfort — Heaven is closed to Him! Man, although he lies dying under the mass of sin, is ungrateful, ignores His love for him! He writhes in profound agony, love submerges Him, tortures Him — His countenance has deathly pallor — His eyes are languid, an indefinable sadness takes entire possession of Him! "My soul is sorrowful unto death."

Divine Blood, spontaneously Thou slowest from the loving Heart of my Jesus; the flood of pain, the extreme bitterness, the steadfast perseverance which He sustains press Thee from that Heart and sweating from His pores Thou dost flow to wash the earth! Let me gather Thee up, Divine Blood, especially these first drops, I want to keep Thee in the chalice of my heart. It is the most convincing proof that love alone has drawn Thee from the veins of my Jesus! I want to purify myself with Thee, and all the places contaminated by sin. I want to offer Thee to the Father.

It is the Blood of His well-beloved Son, who came down to purify the earth; it is the Blood of His Son, the God made flesh, Who ascends to His throne to pacify His justice, offended by our sins. He is superabundantly satisfied.

What am I saying? If the justice of the Father has been satisfied, is Jesus not sated with suffering? No, Jesus does not want to stop the flow of His charity for them. Men must have the infinite proof of His love. He must see to what ignominy it can make Him go. If the infinite justice of the Father is measured by the infinite value of His Most Precious Blood and He is satisfied, man, on his part must have palpable proof that His love is not yet sated with suffering, and that He will not stop, but continue to the extreme agony of the cross, to the ignominious death on it.

Perhaps a spiritually minded man can evaluate, at least in part, the love which reduces Him to the agony of the Garden. But he who lives, given up to material affairs, seeking more the world than Heaven must see Him also agonizing and dying outwardly on the cross, to be moved by the sight of His Blood and of this torturing agony.

No, His loving Heart is not satisfied. Regaining consciousness, He prays again: "Father if Thou dost not wish that this chalice pass from me, unless I drink it, not mine but Thy Will be done."

From now on Jesus responds to the loving cry of His Heart,

to the cry of humanity, which to be redeemed, clamors for His death. At the sentence of death which His Father pronounces against Him, heaven and earth demand His death. Jesus, resigned, bends His adorable head: Father, if Thou dost not want that this chalice passes unless I drink it, not Mine but Thy Will be done."

Behold, He sends an Angel, an Angel-Messenger, to comfort Jesus. What motives of comfort, of relief does the Angel offer to the strong God, Lord of the Universe, the Invincible, the Omnipotent! ... But He has become subject to suffering, He has taken upon himself our weakness; it is the man who suffers and is in agony. It is the miracle of His infinite love which makes him sweat Blood and brings upon Him this agony.

The prayer to His Father has two motives, one for himself, the other for us. His Father does not hear Him for His own sake but wants Him to die for us. I believe that the Angel bows reverently before Jesus, before the Eternal beauty, now covered with blood and dust, and with deferential honor imparts that consolation of resignation of the human will to the Divine Will, beseeching Him for the glory of the Father and in the name of all sinners to drink that chalice which was offered to Him from Eternity for their salvation. He has prayed to teach us also that when our soul finds itself in desolation like His, we should seek consolation from Heaven only in prayer to sustain us in the sacrifice.

He, our strength will be ready to assist us because He had willed to take upon himself our miseries.

Yes, O Jesus, it is for Thee to drink the chalice to the dregs, thou art now vowed to the most terrible death. Jesus, may nothing be able to separate me from Thee, neither life nor death. Following Thee in life, affectionately bound to Thy suffering, may it be granted to me to expire with Thee on the Calvary to ascend with Thee to glory; to follow Thee in tribulations and persecutions, to be made worthy one day to come to love Thee in the unveiled glory of Heaven; to sing to Thee the hymn of thanksgiving for Thy great suffering.

But look! Jesus raises himself from the ground, strong, invincible as a lion in battle; behold now that Jesus, Who longingly had desired this banquet of blood, "with desire have I desired," He shares the disarray from His noble head, wipes the Bloody Sweat from His face, and resolutely goes towards the entrance of the Garden.

Where art Thou going, Jesus? Art Thou not that Jesus I saw languishing in Thy soul, a prey to terror, fatigue, fear, discouragement, desolation? Whom I saw trembling, crushed under the immense weight of the evils which were about to overcome Thee? Where art Thou going now so ready, so resolute, so full of courage? To whom art Thou exposing Thyself?

Oh! I hear it! The weapon of prayer has helped me conquer, and the spirit has subjected the weakness of nature to itself. In prayer have I obtained strength, and now I can face everything. Follow my example and deal with Heaven with the same confidence as I have done.

Jesus approaches the three Apostles. They are still sleeping. Strong emotion, the late hour of the night, that presentiment of something awful — irreparable — which seemed to be approaching, and fatigue, had put them to sleep, such a sleep that weighs down upon one and seems impossible to shake off, and trying to shake it off, one falls into it again without knowing how. Jesus has pity on them saying: "The spirit is willing, but the flesh is weak."

Jesus has so felt this neglect from His own that He exclaims: "Sleep now and rest." He pauses a moment. Suddenly, at the footsteps of Jesus, with an effort they open their eyes. Then Jesus continues: "It is enough. The hour is at hand. The Son of Man will be betrayed into the hands of sinners. Rise, let us go. Behold, he who betrays Me is at hand."

Jesus beholds everything with His all-seeing glance. He seems to say: You who are My friends and disciples sleep, but My enemies are awake and are about to seize Me. You, Peter, who felt strong enough to follow Me unto death, you sleep! From the beginning you gave Me proofs of weakness. But be calm, I clothed Myself with weakness and I have prayed for you, and after you have recognized your mistake, I will be your strength and you will feed My lambs. You, John, also sleep! You, who a few hours past in the ecstasy of My love, have felt the beat of this Heart, you also sleep? Rise, let us go, there is no more time to sleep, the enemy is at the gate; it is the hour of the power of darkness, yes, let us go. I go spontaneously to meet death. Judas hurries to betray Me and I advance with firm and sure step. I will place no obstacle to the fulfillment of the prophecies. My hour has come, the hour of great mercy for humanity.

And in fact, there is heard steps, a reddish light of torches penetrates the Garden and Jesus, followed by the three disciples, advances, intrepid and calm.

CONCLUDING PRAYER

O Jesus, impart to me also that same strength, when my weak nature, foreseeing future evils rebels, so that like Thou, I may accept with serene peace and tranquility all the pains and distress which I may meet on this earth of exile. I unite all to Thy merits, to Thy pains, Thy expiations, Thy tears, that I may cooperate with Thee for my salvation and flee from sin, which was the sole cause of making Thee sweat blood and which led Thee to death. Destroy in me everything that does not please Thee, and with the sacred fire of Thy love write Thy sufferings into my heart. Hold me closely to Thee, with a bond so tight and so sweet, that I shall never again abandon Thee in Thy sufferings.

May I be able to rest on Thy Heart to obtain comfort in the

sufferings of life. May my spirit have no other desire but to live at Thy side in the Garden and unite itself to the pains of Thy Heart. May my soul be inebriated with Thy Blood and feed itself with the bread of Thy sufferings. Amen.

42

Meditation Prayer on Mary Immaculate

Eternal Love, Spirit of Light and Truth, make a way into my poor mind and allow me to penetrate as far as it is possible to a wretched creature like myself, into that abyss of grace, of purity and of holiness, that I may acquire a love of God that is continually renewed, a love of God Who from all eternity planned the greatest of all the masterpieces created by His hands: the Immaculate Virgin Mary.

From all eternity, almighty God took delight in what was to be the most perfect work of His hands and anticipated this wonderful plan with an outpouring of His Grace.

Man, created innocent, fell by disobeying Him; the mark of original sin remained engraved on his forehead and that of his progeny who will bear its consequences until the end of time.

A woman brought ruin, and a woman was to bring salvation. The one, being tempted by a serpent, stamped the mark of sin on the human race; the other was to rise through grace, pure and immaculate. She would crush the head of the serpent who was helpless before her and who struggled in vain under her heel; for she was conceived without sin, and through her came grace to mankind.

Protected with Grace by Him Who was to be the Savior of mankind that had fallen into sin, she escaped all shadow of evil. She sprang from the mind of God as a pure ray of light and will shine like a morning star over the human race that turns to her. She will be the sure guide who will direct our steps toward the

Divine Sun which is Jesus Christ. He makes her radiant with divine splendor and points to her as our model of purity and sanctity. No creature surpasses her, but all the creation defers to her through the Grace of Him who made her immaculate. He Whom she was to carry in her womb was the Son of God, participating with the Father and the Holy Spirit in the glory of her conception.

Clothed in light from the moment of her conception, she grew in grace and comeliness. After almighty God, she is the most perfect of creatures, more pure than the angels. God is indeed well pleased in her since she most resembles Him and is the only worthy repository of His secrets.

In the natural order she preceded her Divine Child, Our Lord, but in the divine order Jesus, the Divine Sun, arose before her; and she received from Him all grace, all purity and all beauty.

All is darkness compared to the pure light that renews a creation through Him Whom she bore in her womb, as the dew on the rose.

The Immaculate Conception is the first step in our salvation. Through this singular and unique gift, Mary received a profusion of Divine Grace, and through her cooperation she became worthy of absorbing infinitely more.

My most pure Mother, my soul so poor, all stained with wretchedness and sin, cries out to your maternal heart. In your goodness deign, I beseech you, to pour out on me at least a little of the grace that flowed into you with such infinite profusion from the Heart of God. Strengthened and supported by this grace, may I succeed in better loving and serving Almighty God who filled your heart completely, and Who created the temple of your body from the moment of your Immaculate Conception.

The Three Divine Persons imbue this sublime creature with all her privileges, her favors and her graces, and with all her holiness.

The Eternal Father created her pure and immaculate and is well pleased in her, for she is the worthy dwelling of His only Son. Through the generating of His Son in His bosom from all eternity, He forecasts of His Son as Man in the pure womb of his mother, and He clothed her from her conception in the radiant snowy garment of grace and of most perfect sanctity; she participates in His perfection.

The Son Who chose her for His Mother poured His wisdom into her that from the very beginning, by infused knowledge, she knew her God. She loved and served Him in the most perfect manner as He never until then had been loved and served on this earth.

The Holy Spirit poured His love into her; she was the only creature worthy or capable of receiving this love in unlimited measure because no other had sufficient purity to come so near to God; and being near to Him she could know and love Him evermore. She was the only creature capable of containing the stream of love which poured into her from on high. She alone was worthy to return to Him from whom came that love. This very love prepared her for that "Fiat" which delivered the world from the tyranny of the infernal enemy and overshadowed her, the purest of doves, making her pregnant with the Son of God.

Oh, my Mother, how ashamed I feel in your presence, weighed down as I am with faults! You are the most pure and immaculate from the moment of your conception, indeed from the moment in eternity when you were conceived in the mind of God.

Have pity on me! May one compassionate look of yours revive me, purify me and lift me up to God; raising me from the filth of this world that I may go to Him who created me, Who regenerated me in Holy Baptism, giving me back my white stole of innocence that original sin had so defiled. Dear Mother, make me love Him! Pour into my heart that love that burned in yours for Him. Even though I will be clothed in misery, I revere the mystery of your Immaculate Conception, and I ardently wish that through it you may purify my heart, so that I may love your God and my God. Cleanse my mind that it may reach up to Him, contemplate Him, and adore Him in spirit and in truth. Purify my body that I too may be a tabernacle for Him and less unworthy of possessing Him when He deigns to come to me in Holy Communion. Amen.

We too, redeemed by Holy Baptism, are corresponding to the grace of our vocation when in imitation of our Immaculate Mother we apply ourselves incessantly to the knowledge of God, in order that we may ever learn better to know Him, to serve Him and to love Him.

43

Prayers

PRAYER AFTER COMMUNION

Stay with me, Lord, for it is necessary to have You present so that I do not forget You. You know how easily I abandon You.

Stay with me, Lord, because I am weak and I need Your strength, that I may not fail so often.

Stay with me, Lord, for You are my life, and without You, I am without meaning and hope.

Stay with me, Lord, for You are my light, and without You, I am in darkness.

Stay with me, Lord, to show me Your will.

Stay with me, Lord, so that I can hear Your voice and follow You.

Stay with me, Lord, for I desire to love You ever more, and to be always in Your company.

Stay with me, Lord, if You wish me to be always faithful to You.

Stay with me, Lord, for as poor as my soul is, I wish it to be a place of consolation for You, a dwelling of Your love.

Stay with me, Jesus, for it is getting late; the days are coming to a close and life is passing. Death, judgment and eternity are drawing near. It is necessary to renew my strength, so that I will not stop along the way, and for that I need You. It is getting late and death approaches. I fear the darkness, the temptations, the dryness, the cross, the sorrows. How I need You, my Jesus, in this night of exile!

Stay with me, Jesus, because in the darkness of this life, with all its dangers, I need You.

Help me to recognize You as Your disciples did at the Breaking of the Bread, so that the Eucharistic Communion be the light which disperses the darkness, the power which sustains me, the unique joy of my heart.

Stay with me, Lord, because at the hour of my death I want to be one with You, and if not by Communion, at least by Your grace and love.

Stay with me, Jesus, I do not ask for divine consolations because I do not deserve them, but I only ask for the gift of Your Presence. Oh, yes! I ask this of You!

Stay with me, Lord, for I seek You alone, Your Love, Your Grace, Your Will, Your Heart, Your Spirit, because I love You and I ask for no other reward but to love You more and more, with a strong and active love.

Grant that I may love You with all my heart while on earth, so that I can continue to love You perfectly throughout all eternity, dear Jesus.

Amen!

PRAYER TO GOD

Lord, God of my heart, You alone know and see all my troubles. You alone are aware that all my distress springs from my fear of losing You, of offending You, from my fear of not loving You as much as I should love and desire to love You.

If You, to whom everything is present and who alone can see the future, know that it is for Your greater glory and for my salvation that I should remain in this state, then let it be so.

I don't want to escape from it. Give me the strength to fight and to obtain the prize due to strong souls.

A BLESSING

May Jesus comfort you in all your afflictions. May He sustain you in dangers, watch over you always with His grace, and indicate the safe path that leads to eternal salvation. And may He render you always dearer to His Divine Heart and always more worthy of Paradise. Amen.

PRAYER TO JESUS

O my Jesus, give me Your strength when my weak nature rebels against the distress and suffering of this life of exile, and enable me to accept everything with serenity and peace.

With my whole strength I cling to Your merits, Your sufferings, Your expiation, and Your tears, so that I may be able to cooperate with You in the work of salvation.

Give me the strength to fly from sin, the only cause of Your agony, Your sweat of blood and Your death.

Destroy in me all that displeases You and fill my heart with the fire of Your holy love and all Your sufferings.

Clasp me tenderly, firmly, close to You that I may never leave You alone in Your cruel Passion. I ask only for a place of rest in Your Heart. Amen.

PRAYER FOR TRUST AND CONFIDENCE IN GOD'S MERCY

O Lord, we ask you for a boundless confidence and trust in Your divine mercy, and the courage to bear the crosses and sufferings which bring immense goodness to our souls and that of Your Church. Help us to love You with a pure and contrite heart, and humble ourselves beneath Your cross, as we climb the mountain of holiness, carrying our cross that leads to heavenly glory. May we receive You with great faith and love in Holy Communion and allow You to act in us as You desire for your greater glory. O Jesus, most adorable Heart and eternal fountain of Divine Love, may our prayer find favor before the Divine Majesty of Your heavenly Father.

44

Humor

In Padre Pio's letters, you'll find helpful advice for your spiritual journey, but also some good humor. Here are a few quotes from volume 3:

Even though you did not send me greetings for my name-day, I thank you just the same. (801)

You are bad, always bad! You are selfish! May Jesus forgive you and be merciful towards you. (790)

May the Lord be merciful to all these souls, my most cordial enemies. ... May the Lord forgive you, not as I have already forgiven you because, frankly, my forgiveness is very labored, but may his pardon be full and complete. (682–683)

That bad Maria has finally written! She will catch it from me when the Lord permits me to see her! (721)

If you truly wish to believe I am a fool, by all means do so, because it doesn't matter, as long as you listen to what I feel I must say to you. (580)

Acknowledgments

I thank Fr. Ronald Giannone, OFM Cap., founder and executive director of the Ministry of Caring. He organized and supervised the publication of this book for the honor of Padre Pio and the glory of God. Padre Pio is immensely proud of the Ministry of Caring's service to the poor of Wilmington, Delaware.

I am grateful to Debbe Philips, chief of staff of the Ministry of Caring, who carefully proofread this manuscript, along with John Sweeney, former editor of the editorial page of the *News Journal* in Wilmington.

I give sincere thanks to my Capuchin brother, Fr. Cyprian Rosen, OFM Cap., as well for his pertinent edits to this book.

Notes

PART 1: PADRE PIO'S JOURNEY
Chapter 1: Padre Pio and the Secular Franciscans
1. Cf. *Letters* 155, 158, 169.
2. Cf. *Letters I*, March 26, 1914.
3. *Letters I*, November 1, 1913.

Chapter 2: One of Us and Yet So Different
1. *Letters I*, June 13, 1919.

Chapter 3: Prophet of Our Time
1. For instance, Letter 394, which Padre Benedetto wrote to Padre Pio from San Marco La Catola on April 5, 1917, gives us a glimpse of Padre Pio's humility. The first observation is the "Piuccio" (little Pius) form used by Padre Benedetto. The suffix "-uccio" denotes particular affection for the person to whom it is addressed.

Chapter 4: Contemplation
1. *Letters I*, November 1, 1913. This letter continues with two more pages. The same topic is described in his letters written on February 9, 1914 (Letter 177), July 16, 1917 (Letter 408), and January 12, 1919 (Letter 522).
2. Ibid., September 4, 1910.
3. The postscript of this letter is in reference to Padre Agostino, who will be his spiritual director after Padre Benedetto. For the sake of clarity, Padre Benedetto did answer to Padre Pio (Letter 18) from San Marco La Catola in September 1910. There was no date on this letter. This dimension of love and pain is also described in the letters of November 29, 1910 (Letter 23), December 20, 1910 (Letter 25), August 10, 1911 (Letter 41), January 13, 1912 (letter 57), March 3, 1912 (Letter 65), March 23, 1912 (Letter 70), June 28, 1912 (Letter 89), December 29, 1912 (Letter 112), October 17, 1915 (Letter 293), November 14, 1917 (Letter 446), and February 26, 1919 (Letter 527).
4. *Letters I*, undated letter of June 1913.
5. For more details, continue reading Letter 131 and also the letters of July 27, 1918 (496), October 17, 1918 (509), March 26, 1914 (184), and January 12, 1919 (520). In the same letter written by Padre Pio to Padre

Benedetto on November 1, 1913, in which he describes the first stage of contemplation (infused supernatural presence), we find also the fourth section of his contemplative life: need of solitude and to be with God alone.

6. *Letters I*, November 1, 1913.

7. Ibid., October 14, 1912.

8. Ibid., June 26, 1913.

9. Ibid., July 16, 1917.

10. Ibid., March 11, 1915. The dark night experience is also mentioned in his Letter 255 on May 20, 1915, to Padre Agostino.

11. Ibid., June 28, 1912.

12. Ibid., October 8, 1920.

13. Ibid., April 2, 1912.

14. St. Augustine, *Confessions*, bk. 10, 29, 40.

15. *Letters I*, September 20, 1912.

16. Ibid., February 16, 1915.

Chapter 5: Humanity and Personality

1. *Letters I*, October 23, 1921.

2. Ibid., June 14, 1920.

3. Ibid., March 26, 1914.

4. Ibid., November 6, 1919.

5. Ibid., June 3, 1921.

6. Ibid. undated letter of January 1912.

7. Ibid., February 28, 1912.

8. Ibid., January 6, 1917.

9. Ibid., September 8, 1911.

10. Ibid., September 18, 1915.

11. See letters dated 5 and 13 of January 1912. His disappointment on this subject and other topic is very clear in the following letters: Letter 141 to Padre Benedetto on July 28, 1913, from Pietrelcina; Letter 285 to Padre Agostino on September 18, 1915, from Pietrelcina; Letter 315 to Padre Agostino on (no date) January 1916, from Pietrelcina; Letter 315 to Padre Agostino on June 14, 1919, from San Giovanni Rotondo; Letter 547 to Padre Benedetto on November 16, 1919, from San Giovanni Rotondo; Letter 613 to Padre Benedetto on October 23, 1921, from San Giovanni Rotondo.

12. *Letters I*, undated letter of January 1912.

13. Ibid., March 14, 1910.

14. Ibid., March 16, 1912.

15. Ibid., December 13, 1912.

16. Ibid., February 27, 1916.

17. Ibid., June 14, 1920.

18. Ibid., March 14, 1910.

19. Ibid., May 26, 1910.

20. Ibid., November 29, 1910.

21. Ibid., October 6, 1911.

22. Ibid., February 25, 1917.

23. Ibid., August 26, 1917.

Chapter 6: The Eucharist

1. *Letters I*, September 8, 1911.

2. It is clear that Padre Pio began writing this letter on March 20 and mailed it on the twenty-first.

3. *Letters I*, August 26, 1917.

4. Ibid., March 29, 1911.

5. Ibid., August 9, 1912.

Chapter 7: The Cross

1. *Letters I*, September 20, 1912.

2. Ibid., February 1, 1913.

3. Ibid., February 13, 1913.

4. Ibid. November 8, 1916.

Chapter 8: The Blessed Mother

1. Fulton J. Sheen, *The World's First Love: Mary, Mother of God* (San Francisco: Ignatius Press, 1996), 13.

2. *Letters I*, May 1, 1912. We actually cannot say what the other grace is which Padre Pio desired. Might it not be the grace to return to community life?

3. Ibid., June 2, 1911.

4. Ibid., July 1, 1915.

Chapter 9: Pray, Hope, and Do Not Worry

1. *Letters I*, September 18, 1915.

2. Ibid., October 4, 1915.

3. Ibid., June 19, 1918.

4. Ibid., August 21, 1918.

5. Ibid., December 29, 1912.

6. Ibid., November 20, 1916.

7. Ibid., July 16, 1917.

8. Ibid., May 4, 1917.

Chapter 10: The Angels

1. *Letters III*, July 2, 1917, 423. Assunta is one of the spiritual daughters.

2. *Letters I*, April 20, 1912.

3. Ibid., May 1, 1912. The quote is from Jer 1:6; the Latin expression means "I do not know how to speak."

4. Ibid., September 7, 1912.

5. Ibid., September 20, 1912.

6. Ibid., October 14, 1912.

7. Ibid., November 5, 1912.

Chapter 11: Humility

1. *Letters I*, October 6, 1911.

2. Ibid., November 1, 1913.

3. Ibid., February 16, 1915.

4. Ibid., April 29, 1919.

5. Ibid., September 6, 1919.

Chapter 12: Isolation and Abandonment

1. *Letters I*, January 1916. The scriptural quote at the end of this letter is in Lk 22:42. Padre Pio did not put any date on this letter, which probably was written on January 20, 1916, and he forgot to sign it. The reason is that he was so overwhelmed by the dark night experience, that everything was void and chaotic around him and within him.

2. Ibid., July 27, 1918.

3. Ibid., July 29, 1910.

4. Ibid., June 24, 1915.

Chapter 13: Poverty

1. *The Constitutions of the Capuchin Friars Minor*, General Curia, 2013, art. 1, 60, 81.

2. Padre Pio left a blank space here!

3. *Letters I*, April 29, 1919.

4. Ibid., March 15, 1913.

5. At that time, the friary was property of the city.

6. *Letters I*, March 21, 1922.

7. Ibid., June 14, 1920.

8. Ibid., June 1920. This letter is undated and has no place of origin.

Chapter 14: Listening Prayer

1. *Catechism of the Catholic Church,* 2567.

2. *Letters I*, October 17, 1915.

Chapter 15: Diabolical Attacks
1. *Letters I*, October 22, 1910.
2. Ibid., November 29, 1910.
3. Ibid., March 29, 1911.
4. Ibid., June 28, 1912.
5. Ibid., November 18, 1912.
6. Ibid., January 18, 1913.
7. Ibid. February 1, 1913.
8. Ibid., February 13, 1913.
9. Ibid., April 8, 1913.

Chapter 16: Temptations
1. *Letters I*, August 17, 1910.
2. Ibid., October 1, 1910.
3. Ibid., March 19, 1911.
4. Ibid., December 20, 1910.
5. For more details on this matter, see Letters 415, 455, and 501.
6. *Letters I*, January 10, 1911.
7. Ibid., June 25, 1911.
8. Ibid., April 1, 1915. The scriptural quotes are taken from Mt 8:25; Mk 4:38; Lk 8:24; see also Mt 14:30.
9. Ibid., May 9, 1915.
10. Ibid., August 4, 1917.
11. Ibid., October 30, 1914.
12. Ibid., March 8, 1916.
13. Ibid., July 16, 1917.
14. Ibid., November 26, 1917.
15. Ibid., December 19, 1917.
16. Ibid., January 24, 1918.

Chapter 17: Obedience
1. *Letters I*, August 15, 1916. "The matter of which you know" was the permission to die.
2. Ibid., January 20, 1921.
3. Ibid. December 18, 1920.
4. Ibid., January 24, 1917.
5. Ibid., June 4, 1918.
6. Ibid., August 21, 1918.

Chapter 18: Call to Holiness
1. Pius XI, *Casti Connubii*, Vatican.va, par. 27.
2. *Letters I*, August 27, 1918.
3. Ibid., September 2, 1911.
4. Ibid., March 17, 1916.
5. Cf. Alessandro da Ripabottoni, *Pio da Pietrelcina: Infanzia e adolescenza*, 3rd ed., 80.
6. *Letters I*, undated letter of June 1913.
7. Ibid., September 20, 1912.
8. Ibid., October 14, 1912.
9. Ibid., December 29, 1912.
10. Ibid., February 1, 1913.
11. Ibid., January 14, 1916.
12. Ibid., November 6, 1919.
13. Ibid., December 18, 1920.
14. Ibid., November 29, 1910.
15. Ibid., November 5, 1912.
16. Ibid., November 18, 1912.
17. Ibid., July 10, 1914.
18. Ibid., March 12, 1913.
19. Ibid., July 27, 1918.

Chapter 19: Mystical Phenomena
1. *Letters I*.
2. Ibid., January 30, 1915.
3. Ibid., May 9, 1915. Similar experiences are described in Letter 293 of October 17, 1915, to Padre Agostino from Pietrelcina, Letter 392 of April 2, 1917, to Padre Benedetto from San Giovanni Rotondo, and Letter 408 of July 16, 1917, to Padre Benedetto from San Giovanni Rotondo.
4. Ibid., December 20, 1918.
5. Ibid., April 18, 1912.
6. Ibid., March 18, 1915.
7. Ibid., March 8, 1916.
8. Ibid., July 27, 1918.
9. Ibid., August 26, 1912. The underlined sentence was written in perfect French language. We know that Padre Pio did not know French at all (see chapter 10, "The Angels"). Similar details about strokes and wounds of love are found in his Letter 82, written to Padre Agostino from Pietrelcina.
10. Ibid., January 24, 1915.
11. Ibid., September 4, 1915.
12. Ibid., August 21, 1918.
13. Ibid., August 27, 1918.

14. Ibid., September 5, 1918.

15. Padre Pio mistakenly gives the wrong date. The right date is September 20.

16. *Letters I*, December 20, 1918.

17. Paolino da Casacalenda, *Le mie memorie intorno a Padre Pio da Pietrelcina*, MS, 131–133.

18. *Letters I*, September 8, 1911.

19. Ibid., March 21, 1912.

20. Ibid. October 22, 1918.

PART 2: SPIRITUAL GUIDANCE
Chapter 20: From Directee to Director

1. *Letters I*, 94.

2. Giovanni da Baggio, *Padre Pio visto dall'interno* [Padre Pio seen from the inside]. *Letters I*, 50.

3. *Letters I*, 107.

4. *Letters III*, lix–lxxv.

5. Ibid., January 12, 1917, to Erminia Gargani, 673.

6. Ibid., September 6, 1916, to Maria Gargani, 253.

7. Ibid., January 27, 1918, to Erminia Gargani, 708.

8. Ibid., January 27, 1918, to Erminia Gargani, 708.

9. Ibid., June 3, 1917, 927. This letter was written to an unidentified person (perhaps Giuseppina or Emanuelina Villani).

10. Ibid., February 2, 1920, to Erminia Gargani, 783.

11. Ibid., October 1, 1917, to Vittorina Ventrella, 611.

12. Ibid., September 4, 1916, to Maria Gargani, 249.

13. Ibid., December 27, 1917, to Maria Gargani, 309. Padre Pio mentions the feast of the beloved disciple, St. John the Evangelist, at the very beginning of the formal greeting.

14. Ibid., May 28, 1917, to Annita Rodote, 110.

15. Ibid., October 1, 1917, to the Ventrella sisters, 574.

16. Padre Benedetto's letter. Cf. *Letters I*, 1136–1137.

17. Letter of May 25 to Nina Campanile.

18. *Letters III*, August 9, 1918, to Assunta Di Tomaso, 434.

19. Ibid., December 6, 1917, to Antonietta Vona, 837.

20. Cf. *Letters I*, 933.

21. *Letters III*, undated letter to Antonietta Vona, 911.

Chapter 22: To Annita Rodote

1. Padre Pio uses this abbreviation in many letters: J(esus), M(ary), J(oseph), D(ominic), F(rancis), C(atherine).

2. Padre signs his letters in different ways: sometimes with Fra or Padre or OFM Cap., Capuchin, Poor son of St. Francis, etc.

Chapter 24: To Maria Gargani

1. The expression "These are a few words" seems to be rhetorical, because Padre Pio wrote two pages about the topic of indifference, which is very good, when it becomes trust and abandonment in God. We know, on the other hand, that indifference can be terrible, if it means skepticism, lack of interest or concern, acceptance of mediocrity. To read the missing part, you may check *Letter* 7, 265 in the third volume of his letters.

Chapter 25: To Assunta Di Tomaso

1. Assunta was twenty-three years old then. It seemed that Padre Pio was suggesting a possible religious vocation. We know that Assunta remained a lay person for the rest of her life.

2. *Letters III*, liv–lv.

Chapter 26: To Lucia Fiorentino

1. Cf. M. Preziosi, *Lucia Fiorentino, figlia spirituale di Parere Pio* (Foggia: 1967), 27–28.

2. Her confessor was Don Giuseppe Massa, about whom Lucia wrote, "He always gave me great encouragement to walk in the ways of the spirit and comforted me greatly in times of physical and moral suffering, however, he didn't always discern God's plan for this soul, which was certainly led along [an] extraordinary path."

3. Taken from the poem "Desiderio del cielo." See Teresa di Gesu, *Opere* (Roma: 1969), 1499.

Chapter 28: To the Ventrella Sisters

1. On March 9, Padre Pio wrote to Padre Benedetto: "For the past three days, I have been deprived of the only comfort I still had in the midst of all my troubles, that is, to be able to go to the Lord's altar to celebrate Mass. For the past three days I have also had a constant fever which shows no signs of diminishing." *Letters I*, 1122.

Chapter 29: To Erminia Gargani

1. These two paragraphs can be read in his letter of February 27 to Padre Agostino. See *Letters I*, 1116.

2. According to the matriculation papers, Padre Pio presented himself on March 5 for military service. See Alessandro da Ripabottoni, *Padre Pio*

da Pietrelcina: "un Cireneo per tutti" (Foggia: 1974), 814.

Chapter 30: To Antonietta Vona
1. N. Campanile, *Memorie su Padre Pio*, MS 1, f. 89.

Chapter 32: To an Unidentified Person
1. Today they are called Secular Franciscans.

2. *Letters III*, 921. For further details, see *Letters I*, 954, note 1; 1004, 1026, 1032.

3. On November 3, Padre Pio wrote to Padre Agostino: "Thanks to the favorable report of the head of this section ... I am being given four months leave. ... I don't know exactly when they'll let me leave, but a few days [may] still be needed. I'll expect your reply in San Giovanni Rotondo, where I'll go as soon as I have been home for a day or two, to get back my religious habit." *Letters I*, 1069.

4. On November 13, Padre Pio wrote to Padre Benedetto from San Giovanni Rotondo. See *Letters I*, 1071.

Chapter 35: To Maria Campanile
1. See Letter 5, dated May 25, 1918, in *Letters III*, 969.

2. See the letter to Padre Benedetto of July 4. *Letters I*, 1146–1150.

3. Girolama was a directee of Padre Pio. She was born in San Giovanni Rotondo, and we have four letters Padre Pio sent to her (see chapter 36).

Chapter 36: To Girolama Longo
1. Girolama Longo's sisters.

2. Margherita Tresca, who entered the Roman Order of the Bridgettines, taking the name of Sr. Maria Benedetta of Jesus.

3. Padre Pio's sister, Sister Pia, born on December 27, 1894, and died on April 30, 1969.

Chapter 37: To Frieda Folger
1. See *Analecta Ord. Fr. Min. Cap.* 70 (1954): 167–169; *Tertius Ordo* 16 (1955): 19–21.

Chapter 38: To Elena Bandini
1. Angelina Serritelli, of San Giovanni Rotondo, a teacher and propagandist for the Secular Franciscans.

Chapter 39: To Violante Masone

1. Graziella Pannullo, a directee of Padre Pio and niece of Don Salvatore Pannullo.

2. Don Salvatore Pannullo, parish priest of Pietrelcina.

3. See *Letters III*, xxix.

4. *Letters II*, 464.

5. Ibid., 553.

6. *Letters III*, xxx.

Chapter 40: To Graziella Pannullo

1. The seventh century of the institution of the Secular Franciscans was celebrated in 1921. See Fredegando Callaey, *Il Terzo Ordine Secolare di San Francesco* (Roma: Saggio Storico, 1921).

2. The Capuchins of the religious Province of Foggia, to which Padre Pio belonged.

3. A. Henrion (Milano: Sorella Chiara, 1921).

4. *Legenda Sanctae Clarae*, n. 15. Cf. Santa Chiara d'Assisi, *La vita e gli scritti*, ed. and trans. Giovanni Casoli (Roma: 1974), 35–36.

5. Ibid., n. 16. Cf. Santa Chiara d'Assisi, *La vita e gli scritti*, 35–36.

About the Author

Fr. John C. Aurilia, OFM Cap., was born in Montemarano, province of Avellino (Campania region) in Italy, on December 8, 1940. He was ordained a priest in 1966, and spent his early years of priesthood teaching at the seminary. For a brief period, he was personal secretary of St. Pio of Pietrelcina. In 1969, he attended the Antonianum University in Rome, Italy, where he was awarded a master of arts degree in philosophy and completed his doctorate in the United States. In 1973, he was called to serve the Italian immigrants in New Jersey. In 1992, he was appointed director of the Catholic Conference Center in Hickory, North Carolina. In 1998, he taught ethics, Italian, and Latin at Don Bosco College in Newton, New Jersey. He was a pastor for many years: in 1993, in Purcellville, Virginia; in 1995, in Hendersonville, North Carolina; in 2003, in Passaic, New Jersey; in 2009, in Tampa, Florida; and in 2015, in the Bronx, New York. In 2022, he was transferred to St. Francis Friary in Wilmington, Delaware.

You might also like:

Padre Pio: The True Story, Revised and Expanded, 3rd Edition
By C. Bernard Ruffin

This is the comprehensive life story of the priest who became world famous for his stigmata, miracles, and supernatural insights. Read in detail about the many miracles of Padre Pio, and discover how knowing this powerful saint can change your life, too.

One of the best biographies of Padre Pio ever written, this third edition is updated with more details and sixteen pages of photos.

Available at
OSVCatholicBookstore.com
or wherever books are sold

You might also like:

Padre Pio's Words of Hope
By Eileen Dunn Bertanzetti

If you've ever wished you could sit down and ask Saint Padre Pio, the famous stigmatist of the 20th century, some of the deepest questions of the human heart, now you can.

With beautiful illustrations and topics ranging from simple queries about the role of angels to the cry of a soul seeking to understand the meaning of suffering, these meditations use the actual words of Padre Pio to answer your most intimate questions and reveal God's own messages of encouragement, exhortation, inspiration, and blessing.

Available at
OSVCatholicBookstore.com
or wherever books are sold